LARAMIE JUNIOR HIGH
SCHOOL LIBRARY

BROKEN PROMISES
The Strange History of the Fourteenth Amendment

If the U.S. Constitution, ever since the Civil War, has promised equal rights for all, why is the fight still continuing today?

In this book the author tells why black Americans have had to struggle for the enforcement of the U.S. Constitution—and how the Fourteenth Amendment has become important in the fight for equal rights for women, for poor people, for all Americans.

BROKEN PROMISES
The Strange History of the Fourteenth Amendment

RICHARD STILLER

Random House 🏠 New York

For helpful suggestions in the preparation of this book, the author and the publisher are grateful to Norman Dorsen, professor of law at New York University, general counsel of the American Civil Liberties Union, and editor of *The Rights of Americans: What They Are, What They Should Be;* and to Charles Harris, executive director, Howard University Press.

PICTURE CREDITS: The Bettmann Archive: 16, 24 left, 27; Black Star: (Ernest Baxter) 112, (Declan Haun) cover, (Flip Schulke) 59, 101; Brown Brothers: 10, 19, 53; Culver Pictures: 9, 12, 14, 28, 33, 37, 40, 44, 65; Historical Pictures Service: 24 right, 69; Library of Congress: 21; Magnum: (Bruce Davidson) 99, (Burt Glinn) 110, (Danny Lyon) 55, 78; New York Historical Society: 6; United Press International: 75, 81, 84, 87, 90, 93, 95; Wide World Photos: 105.

Copyright © 1972 by Richard Stiller

All rights reserved under International and Pan-American Copyright Conventions. Published in the United States by Random House, Inc., New York, and simultaneously in Canada by Random House of Canada Limited, Toronto.

Library of Congress Cataloging in Publication Data
Stiller, Richard. Broken promises.
SUMMARY: Traces the struggle to make the Fourteenth Amendment's promise of equality for all a reality.
Bibliography: p.
1. U. S. Constitution. 14th amendment—History.
[1. U. S. Constitution. 14th amendment—History.
2. Negroes—Civil rights] I. Title.
KF4757.S76   342'.73'085   72-37416
ISBN 0-394-92081-3 (lib. bdg.)

Manufactured in the United States of America

Contents

PROLOGUE	3
The Bloody Spring of 1866	4
The Black Codes	11
For Whites Only	17
Thaddeus Stevens and the Promise of Equality	20
Time of Hope	26
The End of Reconstruction	36
Murder in the Courtroom	39
The Triumph of Jim Crow	51
A New Leadership for Blacks	63
The NAACP Campaigns for the Fourteenth Amendment	77
The End of "Separate but Equal"	85
Putting Teeth in the Right to Be Equal	92
Everybody's Fourteenth Amendment	100
Unfinished Business	109
APPENDIX: The Fourteenth Amendment	114
BIBLIOGRAPHY	116
INDEX	118

BROKEN PROMISES

Prologue

Frederick Douglass, America's most distinguished black man, stood in the crowd and watched Abraham Lincoln take the oath of office for his second term. The President noticed Douglass and pointed him out to the new Vice President, Andrew Johnson of Tennessee.

Johnson glanced over at Douglass. The black leader noted the Vice President's reaction. "The first expression which came to his face," Douglass later wrote, "was one of bitter contempt and aversion. Seeing that I observed him, he tried to assume a more friendly appearance, but it was too late."

Six weeks later Lincoln was dead. Andrew Johnson became President of the United States.

The Bloody Spring of 1866

In March of 1866 the Civil War had been over for almost a year. Four million black people, formerly slaves, were now "free." But in the South the white men who had started and lost the war intended to remain masters over their former slaves. An Alabama planter spoke for most of them when he told a visiting newspaperman: "The nigger is going to be made into a serf."

Blacks had some friends in Congress—the Radical Republicans. To give blacks equal rights with whites, these Senators and Congressmen wrote and passed the Civil Rights Act of 1866.

The idea of equality was not mentioned in the United States Constitution. But now this new law said:

> All persons born in the United States . . . are hereby declared to be citizens of the United States; and such citizens, of every race and color, . . . shall have the same right, in every State and Territory in the United States, . . . as is enjoyed by white citizens.

For the first time in American history black people were declared by federal law to be citizens of the

United States. More important, the new law specifically made them the equal of white citizens.

And then, on March 27, President Johnson vetoed the Civil Rights Act. It was not proper, he said in his message to Congress, "to make our entire colored population . . . citizens of the United States."

President Johnson's veto was the signal for violence and murder all over the South. His message to Congress reaffirmed the point of view that blacks had no rights—and that a white man could commit any crime against them. The law would not stop such crimes. The law was for the protection of white people only.

In Memphis, Tennessee, the mayor, the sheriff, and the attorney general organized a conspiracy of city policemen. They intended to kill black soldiers who were living at nearby Fort Pickering while they awaited discharge from the Union Army. The conspirators would get the help of some city firemen and of a white mob from Arkansas. As later reported to Congress, the attack started on Tuesday afternoon, May 1.

Most of the black soldiers heard about the plot in time to protect themselves inside Fort Pickering. The police mob—armed with rifles, shotguns, derringers, revolvers, and bowie knives—turned, in their rage, on every black person they could find.

Jackson Goodell, a 27-year-old wagon driver, was among the first to die.

He had stopped in a grocery store on his way home

Black riflemen of the U.S. Army. About 200,000 served with Northern troops during the Civil War.

from work. It was his bad luck to find two policemen there. They drew their revolvers and shot at him. But he turned and ran—ran out of the store and around the corner, directly into a mob led by a police sergeant on horseback.

The sergeant rose in his stirrups and screamed: "Kill him! Kill the nigger, all the God-damned niggers!" The two policemen on foot caught up with Goodell and clubbed him down. Later his wife Lavinia found his body on the floor of the police station. The police refused to give it back for a decent funeral.

In another part of Memphis, 16-year-old Taylor Hunt was walking home to dinner. He worked for a rich white man and got paid cash. Until the age of 13 he had worked in the fields for nothing, because he had been a slave. But then the war came and ended slavery.

Taylor Hunt saw a policeman and another white man walking toward him. He knew he had done nothing wrong. As the two white men came by, the policeman raised his gun and shot Taylor in the head.

Taylor was lucky. The bullet did not kill him. It only made a mess of the side of his face. He lay in the street, his eyes drowning in blood. He couldn't see, but he could feel and hear. He felt the cold revolver against his ear. He heard a rough growl.

"Are you a soldier?"

"No," said Taylor.

"Damned good thing you're not."

The gun went away. The growl ended. Footsteps went off down the cobblestones. He was alone. He was alive.

Fayette Dickerson was a few years older than Taylor—old enough to be a trooper in the 15th Colored Infantry. Unfortunately he was wearing his uniform. As he was seriously wounded in the head and stomach, he heard a white man shout: "That will teach you to leave your old master!"

Seven policemen broke into the house of Bob Taylor, a soldier in the 59th Regiment. He was already on his way to Fort Pickering. But his sister Lucy and her two babies were in the house. The policemen raped Lucy and took her money. Members of the mob raped five more black women that day and the next. Some they set fire to.

Later the mob found Bob Taylor before he could get to Fort Pickering and murdered him in the street. It wasn't until Saturday that the under-strength 16th United States Infantry stationed at Fort Pickering—only 150 soldiers—could restore order in the city. By then the mob's bloody work had been done.

Forty-six black people were dead, including 13 women and two children. Two whites—a policeman and a fireman—were also killed. Four black churches and twelve schools for black children were burned down. White ministers, white teachers, and other white people friendly to blacks and loyal to the Union were chased out of Memphis.

Major General George Stoneman, commander in chief at Fort Pickering, reported to Congress that the United States flag could be flown at only three locations in Memphis—at his military headquarters, at the Freedmen's Bureau, and at the office of the *Memphis Post,* a newspaper loyal to the Union. A mill owner who tried to fly the Stars and Stripes was warned to pull it down or have his mill burned down. In Memphis theaters, audiences hissed "The Star-Spangled Banner."

The general praised the behavior of his troops. But his small force was barely able to uphold law and order against the police and their mob of supporters. The men who had owned slaves were in power again.

Another police massacre took place in New Orleans. Again the mayor and the police and a secret band of white terrorists—the Knights of the White

During the Memphis riot, local policemen and a white mob attacked any blacks they could find. This drawing appeared in a national magazine a few weeks later.

Camelia—were the attackers. The victims were black and white delegates to a convention called to draw up a new constitution for the state of Louisiana. The new constitution was to give black men the right to vote.

Breaking into the hall where the meeting was being held, the attackers shot and clubbed the delegates there. Before United States troops arrived, 40 people were murdered, 36 of them black. Another 150 were wounded.

The new state constitution—and the right of blacks to vote in Louisiana—were dead, too.

About a thousand people, almost all of them black, died in the bloody spring of 1866. As the Memphis

Frederick Douglass, runaway slave and leading abolitionist before the Civil War, was a spokesman for black rights after the war.

mob told United States officials and black leaders: "By God, we will clean you all out! Just get the troops away and we'll show you, when we get things into our own hands!"

Black veterans held meetings of protest. In Alexandria, Virginia, a convention of blacks asked Congress to keep United States soldiers in the Southern states "until you have so amended the Federal Constitution that it will prohibit the states from making any distinction between citizens on account of race or color."

In Boston, Frederick Douglass told an audience that slavery was not dead; it had just changed its shape. "Wait and see," he said, "what new form this old monster will assume; in what new skin this old snake will come forth."

But the time for waiting was past. The snake had come forth. Someone would have to kill it. Since the President wouldn't, it was up to Congress.

The Black Codes

Even before the bloody spring of 1866, Congress was aware that there were problems in the South. During 1865, shortly after the Civil War ended, stories of mistreatment of former slaves began to reach Congress.

There was the story of Joseph Wiggins, a black teenager in Beaufort County, North Carolina. A Boston man returning from a Southern trip told the story to a Pennsylvania Congressman.

Young Joseph Wiggins was still held as a slave by a man named Roddick Carney. Joseph's family lived nearby. Mr. Wiggins was a well-respected member of the community. But he could do nothing to free his son.

When Mr. Wiggins went to the police they laughed at him. When he went to the county courthouse the officials told him they could do nothing. He was just a black man. Black men had no rights.

Roddick Carney kept the boy in chains and used him as a slave. Carney was a cruel, dangerous man. Just for the fun of it, to show his marksmanship, he

Selling a black man in Florida to pay a fine—after the Civil War.

had shot and killed two other black teenagers from nearby Pitt County.

Mr. Wiggins went to the United States Army. The Army sent a detachment of soldiers to free Joseph. But Carney and his friends were waiting—with guns. They fought off the soldiers, killing an Army lieutenant in the battle.

Joseph Wiggins was still a slave.

There were other stories, tales of murder and torture. White men in the South behaved as if black men were not citizens. And in fact they were not. According to the Thirteenth Amendment to the Constitution, they were *free*. But they could not vote, serve on juries, or give testimony against white men in trials. Nor could they enjoy any of the legal or police protection that real citizens—white men—enjoyed.

During 1865 the Southern states passed new laws called Black Codes which had the effect of preventing black people from moving off the plantations. The Black Codes restricted their movements and forced them to work for their masters at whatever wages the masters wanted to pay them.

According to some Black Codes they could be arrested and fined for petty "offenses" like drinking, loud talking, or being "rude" to white people. If a black had no money to pay his fine—and most of the newly freed blacks had no money at all—he was sold to any white man who paid the fine to the county. The white man could then work the black man for a long enough time to pay off the money he had spent. The sheriff would make sure that the black man did not run away.

In Maryland the sheriff of Anne Arundel County put up a public notice:

> The undersigned will sell at the courthouse door, in the city of Annapolis, at twelve o'clock Saturday . . . a Negro man named Richard Harris, for six months, convicted . . . for larceny, and sentenced by the court to be sold as a slave. Terms of sale, cash.

This was slavery all over again. Southern white people did not try to hide the fact. They thought it the most natural thing in the world for blacks to be slaves of whites. They believed that all black people belonged to all white people.

The reports from the South angered people in the North, especially Republicans. Was this what the

14 *The Black Codes*

North had fought and won the war for? Was this why two-thirds of a million men had died?

Yet not everybody in the North was moved by sympathy for blacks. Except in five New England states, Northern blacks could not vote either. In most Northern states, blacks were discriminated against. They did not have the same rights of citizenship as whites.

But most Americans of the North and West resented the power and arrogance of the defeated Southern rebels. The white Southerners had been trai-

A young black woman being whipped by a white mob in North Carolina in 1867.

tors to the United States—and now they abused blacks who supported the United States government! Pressed by mounting public anger, President Andrew Johnson agreed to send Carl Schurz on a fact-finding trip through the South. Schurz was a Republican leader who had been a Union general during the Civil War.

Schurz found facts that were even more terrible than the stories that had alarmed the North. He reported:

> Violent efforts were made by white people to drive the . . . Negroes back to the plantations by force. . . . I saw in various hospitals Negroes, women as well as men, whose ears had been cut off or whose bodies were slashed with knives or bruised with whips or bludgeons, or punctured with shot wounds. Dead Negroes were found in considerable number in the country roads or on the fields, shot to death, or strung upon limbs of trees.

Carl Schurz concluded: "People . . . are yet unable to conceive of the Negro as possessing any rights at all."

The Schurz report added to the anger and resentment in the North. By the time the Thirty-ninth Congress met in early December, 1865, Republican Congressmen were bombarded with demands to do something to help the blacks and crush the ex-rebels.

There were demands to give black men the right to vote. There were demands to put the ex-Confederate leaders in jail, or at least to keep them out of office.

Congressman Thaddeus Stevens, who fought for true equality for Southern blacks.

(The Thirty-ninth Congress refused to seat representatives from the Southern states.) There were demands to send an army of occupation to govern the Southern states until white people there demonstrated their loyalty to the United States.

The Quaker poet John Greenleaf Whittier expressed these demands in his poem "To The Thirty-ninth Congress":

> Make all men peers before the law,
> Take hands from off the Negro's throat,
> Give black and white an equal vote.

Radical Republican Congressmen led by Thaddeus Stevens of Pennsylvania agreed. They were determined to stop the Southern terror. But there was a serious obstacle to equal rights for blacks. That obstacle was the Constitution of the United States.

For Whites Only

The U.S. Constitution, the basic law of the land, discriminated against black people even though it never used the word "slave" or "slavery."

When it was adopted in 1789, the Constitution protected slavery. Many of the men who wrote the Constitution were themselves owners of slaves. Even a liberal Northerner like Benjamin Franklin had once owned a Negro slave. All of the Founding Fathers, including Thomas Jefferson who also owned slaves, believed that black men were inferior to white men. When they said in the Declaration of Independence that all men were created equal, they meant all *white* men.

When the Constitution referred to black people it did not call them "citizens," as it did white people. It referred to them as "all other persons" or "persons held to service or labor."

The Constitution allowed each Southern state to use three-fifths of the total number of "all other persons" as a basis for figuring additional Congressmen from the state. This was almost the same as saying that a black man was only three-fifths of a white man.

The Constitution even protected the right of the states to import slaves. It said that until 1808 Congress could not pass a law which would stop anyone from bringing slaves into the country.

Worst of all, the Constitution had said that if a slave ran away from his master to a free state, it was the duty of that state to catch him and ship him back to slavery.

Just four years before the Civil War, the Supreme Court put the finishing touches on the degradation of the black man. In the *Dred Scott Case,* the Court ruled that Negroes "are not included and were not intended to be included under the word 'citizen' in the Constitution." Negroes, said Supreme Court Chief Justice Roger B. Taney, "had no rights which the white man was bound to respect."

Both the Constitution and the Supreme Court said: *Negroes are not citizens. They have no rights.*

In December, 1865, the Thirteenth Amendment changed the Constitution sufficiently to end slavery. But that didn't make black people citizens. It was clear to many people that the Constitution would have to be changed again. Another amendment, a fourteenth, would have to be passed.

Passing amendments is difficult. An amendment, in addition to being approved by two-thirds of the House and Senate, has to be ratified by three-fourths of the states.

Passing a law is easier. All that is required is ap-

Dred Scott. Four years before the Civil War, the Supreme Court ruled in his case that blacks had no rights under the Constitution.

proval by more than half the House and Senate, and the signature of the President. But a law can be declared unconstitutional by the Supreme Court. An amendment can't; it becomes *part* of the Constitution.

All through December and into the spring of 1866 the Republican leaders argued and worked over an amendment that would guarantee black people their citizenship and their political rights.

During that bloody spring of 1866, after the President's veto of the Civil Rights Act, the massacres in Memphis and New Orleans backfired. They shocked the North into supporting stronger measures against the South. Congress repassed the Civil Rights Act of 1866 by a two-thirds majority (no longer requiring the President's signature) and made it a law.

And then in June, Congress passed the Fourteenth Amendment to the Constitution and sent it to the states for ratification.

Thaddeus Stevens and the Promise of Equality

In his heart of hearts Congressman Thaddeus Stevens didn't have much confidence that the new amendment would be able to protect black people in the South.

All his life he had been a lawyer and a legislator. Starting as an ordinary politician from Lancaster, Pennsylvania, he had become the most influential man in the House of Representatives. Some people thought he was the most powerful man in Washington.

Thaddeus Stevens was 74 now. He had spent a good part of his life fighting for Negro rights. It began back in 1836 when he was a much younger man. Somewhere in those years he had lost confidence in laws, in words scratched on paper. He had become suspicious, especially of the Southern planters.

Stevens did not really think the black man would be free, no matter how many laws were passed, until he had power. And he would never have power until he had land. The white planters had power over the blacks because they owned the land and the blacks

Five generations of a black family in Beaufort, South Carolina. Some Radical Republicans wanted to give land to families like this so that they would be economically independent.

owned nothing. The blacks could not eat unless the white masters hired them and paid them.

In such a set of circumstances, giving black men the right to vote or the other rights of citizenship would not be sufficient to make black people equal with whites. What could a starving man, a powerless man, do with the right to vote or the right to sit on a jury or the right to testify in court?

Stevens was one of those few white men who truly wanted black people to achieve equal rights with white people. He was a bitter enemy of the white Southern landowners. He dreamed of a South populated by independent black and white farmers instead of the South as it was, controlled by a handful of rich white landowners who did little work themselves.

Stevens wanted to take the vast plantations away from the white planters and divide them up so that every black man would get a free gift of a farm of 40 acres. The rest of the millions of acres would be sold to poor Southern white men at low prices. This, said Stevens, would change the South into a real democracy. If such an act drove the rich planters out of the country, Thaddeus Stevens would say "good riddance."

"If they go, all the better," he declared. "It is easier and more beneficial to exile seventy thousand proud, bloated, and defiant rebels than to expatriate four million laborers, native to the soil and loyal to the Government."

Hardly anybody agreed with him. Northern leaders were not pleased with the idea of taking property away from Southerners, because they were property owners themselves. If the government took plantations away from Southern planters today, might they not take railroads, mines, and factories away from Northern capitalists tomorrow? Republican Party leaders shuddered at that.

Sadly, Stevens forgot about taking land away from the planters and led the successful fight for passage of the Fourteenth Amendment.

This amendment has been called the Magna Charta of black people. The amendment's important first section starts out with words very much like those in the Civil Rights Act of 1866:

> All persons born or naturalized in the United States, and subject to the jurisdiction thereof, are citizens of the United States and of the State wherein they reside. No State shall make or enforce any law which shall abridge the privileges or immunities of citizens of the United States; nor shall any State deprive any person of life, liberty, or property without due process of law; nor deny to any person within its jurisdiction the equal protection of the laws.

By these words blacks were declared American citizens. The extremely important last phrase of that section guaranteed them "the equal protection of the laws." That phrase meant that racial discrimination by any state government was forbidden.

There was another important section of the Fourteenth Amendment. This was the fifth and last section, which said: "The Congress shall have power to enforce, by appropriate legislation, the provisions of this article." This gave Congress the right to pass any law that seemed necessary in order to make the Fourteenth Amendment work.

The right to vote was not included in the Fourteenth Amendment. Despite Stevens' personal wishes,

Senator Charles Sumner, 12 years before the Civil War, tried unsuccessfully to end segregated schools in Boston—the home of abolition.

the opposition among Democrats and conservative Republicans was too strong at this time.

Among the Radical Republicans who wanted blacks to have this right, there was grumbling and dissatisfaction. Senator Charles Sumner of Massachusetts at first opposed the amendment outright because it did not give blacks the vote. He called it "another compromise with human rights." But then in the end he supported it, although grudgingly.

The Fourteenth Amendment *did* say that if any state prevented some of its male citizens over 21 from voting, the state would lose some of its Congressmen in the House of Representatives. This was to permit Southern states a choice. If a state let black men vote, it would lose nothing. If it didn't let black men vote, it would have to pay the penalty of reduced representation in Congress. (No state has ever paid this penalty, even though Southern states have prevented blacks from voting for more than a hundred years. *This part of the amendment has never been enforced.*)

Congress did one more thing. It passed a law requiring each Southern state to ratify the Fourteenth Amendment before it could come back into the Union and elect members to Congress.

Until the Southern states did that, the United States Army would remain in the South to see that black people were protected—and that the state governments did not pass any more Black Codes.

Like all laws, the Fourteenth Amendment was no more than words on paper. But these were very important words. They committed the government of the United States to a solemn promise—a promise of full freedom and equality to all citizens, black and white. It was a promise by the federal government to intervene if any state did not treat all its citizens equally.

In July of 1868, when the Fourteenth Amendment was officially declared a part of the Constitution, it looked as if racism sustained by law was dead in the United States.

Time of Hope

A few weeks later Thaddeus Stevens died. He did not live long enough to see how well the promise of the Fourteenth Amendment was kept.

For a time it looked as if the United States government would keep its promise.

In the late 1860s and early 1870s democracy began to take slow root in the South. The United States Army patrolled the cities and towns to make sure that white Southerners obeyed the Civil Rights Act of 1866, as well as the new Reconstruction Acts passed under its authority and that of the Fourteenth Amendment. These acts, passed by Congress, required the states to protect the civil rights of all citizens.

Congress also passed the Fifteenth Amendment, the last of the three Civil War amendments, and required the Southern states to ratify it. This amendment guaranteed voting rights to all citizens without regard to race or color. It was another promise by the United States government to black Americans. When the Fifteenth Amendment was ratified in 1870, close

Enforcing black rights during Reconstruction: U.S. Army troops in the South Carolina state capitol ten years after the Civil War.

to three-quarters of a million new black voters were thus added to the election rolls in the South.

And these new black citizens voted under the protection of the Army. Together with their white fellow Southerners they elected progressive new officials in the states that used to practice slavery. These new office holders, many of them blacks, represented the interests of all Southern people and not just the interests of a few rich planters.

The new state governments adopted new constitutions. All of these new constitutions guaranteed the

28 *Time of Hope*

right to vote to all male citizens over 21 regardless of how poor they were.

The new state governments did something else that was important: they set up free public-school systems. The ex-slaves knew the value of education. They knew that their children could have a decent future only if they had a decent education. Poor white Southerners also wanted free education for their chil-

Blacks and whites working together in the South Carolina state legislature during Reconstruction.

dren. In the North a poor white family could have that, but in the South before the Civil War there was no public-school system. Only the children of well-to-do white parents received an education.

In Louisiana the state constitution provided that new public schools must be integrated (though in fact very few black children went to school with white children). But even where Southern black children went to separate schools, as much money was spent on their education as on the education of white children.

It was a time when education meant a great deal in the South. In its first year of public education, Mississippi spent more on the schooling of its children than on all other government activities put together.

For a few years Negroes held office widely in the South. Fourteen blacks were elected to the United States House of Representatives. Mississippi sent two black men to Washington as Senators: Hiram Revels and Blanche Bruce. Louisiana elected three black lieutenant governors, South Carolina two, and Mississippi one. Florida had a black Secretary of State who later became head of the state's public-school system.

But in fact Reconstruction was a fragile flower. It did not sink strong roots in the minds and hearts of most white Southerners. Its major support was the United States Army, whose soldiers occupied the South.

Senator Charles Sumner of Massachusetts doubted the permanence of Reconstruction. He did not think the Fourteenth Amendment went far enough. He did not trust his fellow white Americans to be sufficiently sensitive to Negro rights. He wanted to erect a wall of laws to protect those rights.

In 1870 he tried to get Congress to pass a new civil-rights act. This new law would forbid racial segregation in hotels, theaters, on juries, in churches, in cemeteries, and—most important—in schools.

Black newspapers campaigned for the bill. A black Congressman from South Carolina told the House of Representatives: "All we ask is . . . a law so strong and powerful that no one will be able to elude it and destroy our rights under the Constitution."

At first Congress refused to pass Sumner's bill. The Senator died, defeated, in 1874. But the next year the Republicans were able to get the bill passed with some changes.

This important Civil Rights Act of 1875 was passed under the authority of the Fourteenth Amendment. It made segregation in public facilities—such as hotels, restaurants, and railroads—a federal offense. Under this law it was illegal to discriminate against any United States citizen in the use of public facilities. The penalty was a fine of from $500 to $1000 plus a jail sentence.

A few months later a black man named Bird Gee sat down at a table in Murray Stanley's hotel dining room in Topeka, Kansas.

"What do you want?" asked the waiter coldly.

"I want to order dinner," replied Mr. Gee. "Bring me a menu."

"Mr. Stanley doesn't serve colored people," said the waiter.

Bird Gee did not waste any time arguing. He went straight to the United States District Attorney and charged Murray Stanley with violation of the law. The District Attorney agreed that the restaurant owner had broken the law—the Civil Rights Act of 1875. Six months later a federal grand jury handed down an indictment. Stanley was accused of the federal crime of denying the "privileges of an inn to a person of color."

But Stanley's lawyers argued in court that the Civil Rights Act of 1875 was unconstitutional. They said that the Fourteenth Amendment did not give Congress the authority to pass a law concerning racial discrimination in public places.

The federal District Attorney argued that the Fourteenth Amendment *did* give Congress that authority. He quoted the amendment's famous "equality" clause: "No State shall . . . deny to any person within its jurisdiction the equal protection of the laws."

Those words, said the District Attorney, meant that it was the duty of the government to see that all its citizens, black as well as white, were treated equally. In passing the Civil Rights Act of 1875, Congress was doing its constitutional duty.

For some reason the federal court in Kansas couldn't make up its mind. Perhaps the judges did not really think racial discrimination ought to be illegal. They turned the case over to the court that has the final word in such matters: the Supreme Court of the United States. The Supreme Court put the case of *United States v. Stanley* to one side and turned its attention to matters that it thought more important. In the meantime Bird Gee would have to eat dinner someplace else. Murray Stanley could continue to discriminate against black people until the Supreme Court told him to stop.

Other cases of racial discrimination were arising in the late 1870s. But they were not too frequent. In those days not a single state had laws requiring separation of whites and blacks. Most white people took the Fourteenth Amendment seriously even if they did not agree with it.

A few individual theater owners or hotel owners refused to serve black customers. But these were the exception. Most public facilities served blacks equally with whites. Some sold first-class railroad or theater tickets to whites only, or to whites and wealthy blacks. But they allowed other blacks to share second-class facilities with white customers on an equal basis. Three Northern states and several Southern states had passed their own civil-rights laws forbidding discrimination in public accommodations.

In some cases where whites tried to discriminate against blacks, the blacks fought back and won. In Louisville, Kentucky, they successfully resisted an attempt to make them ride on the outside platforms of streetcars. Individual blacks went to court for their rights when they were treated unfairly, just as Bird Gee did.

Thomas Wentworth Higginson, an old radical abolitionist, traveled through the South to see for himself how black people were treated. Higginson had been an aggressive fighter against slavery. He had been the commanding officer of the first black regiment in the United States Army. He was strongly biased against the white South and in favor of black citizens.

To his astonishment he found that blacks were often treated as fairly in public places as in his native Massachusetts. In the South, blacks rode the trains

During Reconstruction, J. J. Wright was a judge of the state supreme court in Columbia, South Carolina.

and streetcars equally with whites. Reconstruction accomplished that much, at least.

A distinguished English visitor was impressed with the freedom with which black and white people associated on public vehicles. He wrote that "the humblest black rides with the proudest white on terms of perfect equality and without the smallest symptom of malice or dislike on either side."

Another observer wrote of Columbia, South Carolina: "The negroes are freely admitted to the theatre . . . and to other exhibitions, lectures, etc. . . . In Columbia they are also served at the bars, soda water fountains, and ice-cream saloons."

On the other hand, Murray Stanley was not the only white who refused to serve black customers. There were other proprietors who were racially prejudiced.

In New York City, the Grand Opera House refused to admit William R. Davis for a performance by the famous actor Edwin Booth. Davis was a black man, a representative of a black weekly newspaper.

In Jefferson City, Missouri, the Nichols House refused to accept W. H. R. Agee, a black man, as a guest.

In San Francisco, Michael Ryan, doorkeeper at Maguire's Theatre, refused to accept the ticket of George M. Tyler.

And in Tennessee, Mrs. Sallie J. Robinson was forced by a conductor of the Memphis and Charleston Railroad to leave the parlor car and sit in the smoking car. The conductor called Mrs. Robinson "girl" and said: "Why do you people try to force yourself in that car?"

In these four cases of discrimination, the United States government charged the proprietors with violating the Civil Rights Act. The proprietors were all tried and found guilty. Like Murray Stanley, they all appealed to the Supreme Court.

In Louisiana a mob of white men broke up meetings of black citizens, and beat and threatened black men who tried to vote. The members of the mob were arrested and tried in federal court for violating one of the Reconstruction Acts passed by Congress under the authority of the Fourteenth Amendment.

The Louisiana terrorists were found guilty. They too appealed to the Supreme Court.

Black and white Americans waited to see what the Supreme Court would do.

The End of Reconstruction

The hopeful period of Reconstruction did not last very long. Too many white Southerners were unable to think of black people as their equals. Bands of white terrorists—the Ku Klux Klan—controlled the Southern countryside, where most Southerners lived.

As the 1870s wore on, the Army, the Congress, and the people of the North grew weary and indifferent—tired of what they called "the Negro problem." The Civil War was long over. People in the North were more interested in making money than in protecting black people's rights far away in the South.

Thaddeus Stevens and Charles Sumner and most of the old anti-slavery men were gone from Congress. Some former abolitionists turned against the black man. "Slavery is dead," they said. "Black men are legally free. What more do they want?"

In 1876 the Republican Party of the North made a "deal" with the Democratic Party of the South. There had been a bitter dispute over the results of the Presidential election of that year. Finally the Democrats agreed to support the Republican candidate, Rutherford B. Hayes, for President. In return, Hayes and the other Republicans agreed to end Reconstruction by withdrawing the U.S. Army from the South.

Once the Army departed, blacks and the Reconstruction state governments in the Southern states were at the mercy of the Ku Klux Klan.

When Reconstruction ended, U.S. Army troops no longer protected Southern blacks. This drawing (showing the initials of the Ku Klux Klan scratched on a wall) was called "One Vote Less."

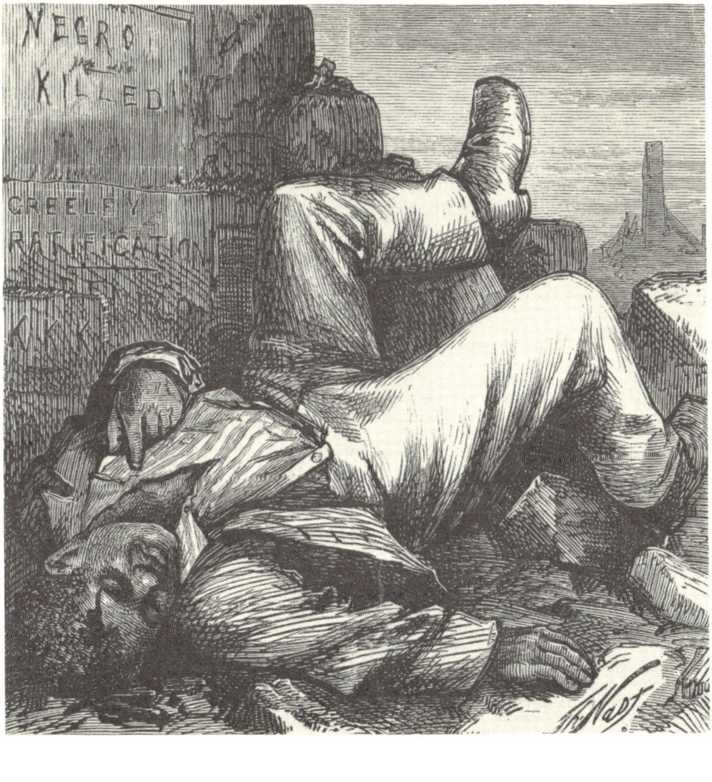

The End of Reconstruction

Black people now fought pitched battles to defend themselves against armed white mobs all across the South. But the blacks were surrounded and outnumbered. Black men were shot trying to vote. Black lawmakers were driven out of office. White men who allied themselves with blacks were chased out of the South, their homes burned, their families threatened. It was the bloody spring of 1866 all over again.

Former Senator Benjamin Franklin Wade of Ohio, a lifelong anti-slavery man and Radical Republican leader, wrote to the New York *Times*: "I have been deceived, betrayed, and humiliated by [President Hayes]. . . . I feel that to have emancipated those people and then to leave them unprotected would be a crime."

Reconstruction was over. The United States Army no longer protected blacks in the South.

But the Civil Rights Acts of 1866 and 1875 were part of the law of the land. The Fourteenth Amendment was part of the Constitution. Its words guaranteed black citizens equal rights and freedom from racial discrimination and segregation.

Or did they?

Murder in the Courtroom

When there is a disagreement about the meaning of the United States Constitution or one of its amendments, it is up to the Supreme Court to interpret the Constitution.

From 1868 on, the Fourteenth Amendment was part of the Constitution. Its language seemed to be clear. The amendment said that Negroes were citizens and had all the rights white men had. The men in Congress who had worked and argued over it believed they were hammering out a declaration of independence for blacks.

The very first time the Supreme Court considered a case involving the Fourteenth Amendment, the Court said that the purpose of the amendment was "the freedom of the slave race." The Court added that the amendment's "main purpose was to establish the citizenship of the Negro."

But that was in 1873, during the hopeful days of Reconstruction. By 1876 public opinion had changed. So had the Supreme Court.

The Court had always been conservative. By 1876

seven of its nine justices were Northerners more interested in protecting the new business corporations than in protecting the rights of the former slaves. The other two were Southerners. None of the nine had been anti-slavery men.

Some of the Court's justices were racists. One of these was Stephen J. Field. When the Court majority decided in 1873 that the purpose of the Fourteenth Amendment was the protection of Negro rights, Jus-

Armed whites massacred black voters in Colfax, Louisiana, in 1873. This drawing in a national magazine showed survivors gathering the dead and wounded.

tice Field disagreed. He wrote to a friend: "I belong to the class who repudiate the doctrine that this country was made for the people of *all* races. On the contrary, I think it is for our race—the Caucasian race." In the hands of men like Justice Field, what would happen to the Fourteenth Amendment? In 1876—the same year that the Republicans and the Democrats came to their agreement to end Reconstruction—the Supreme Court gave part of its answer to that question. The Court was hearing the case of the Louisiana terrorists who had been found guilty of violating the civil rights of black citizens. The case was called *United States v. Cruikshank.*

By a unanimous vote the Supreme Court now reversed the judgment of the federal court in Louisiana—and set the white men free. The Court said: "The Fourteenth Amendment . . . adds nothing to the rights of one citizen as against another."

Yet Congress had written the amendment in order to do just that—to give black people rights they never had under the Constitution. Now the Supreme Court was saying the exact opposite.

The Court also said that the Fourteenth Amendment protected black people from the actions of state governments but *not* from the actions of private citizens. Since the Louisiana mob was made up of private citizens, the Court ruled that the Fourteenth Amendment did not protect the blacks from murder and violence in this case.

The Fourteenth Amendment was only eight years old. Already the Supreme Court was weakening it, saying it did not mean what Thaddeus Stevens and the other men who had written it had meant it to mean.

Seven years later, in 1883, the Supreme Court took up the case that the Kansas federal court had not decided. Was restaurant owner Murray Stanley guilty of discriminating against Bird Gee in violation of the Civil Rights Act of 1875?

To the case of Murray Stanley the court added the cases of the four other white-owned establishments charged with racial discrimination:

(1) The case of the New York Grand Opera House, which refused to admit William R. Davis—because he was black.

(2) The case of the Missouri hotel which refused to rent a room to W. H. R. Agee—because he was black.

(3) The case of the San Francisco theater which refused to sell a ticket to George M. Tyler—because he was black.

(4) And the case of the Memphis and Charleston Railroad, whose conductor put Mrs. Sallie J. Robinson out of the parlor car—because she was black.

Since all five cases concerned the Civil Rights Act of 1875, they were put before the Supreme Court under the title *Civil Rights Cases*. The Court ruled almost eight years to the day after Bird Gee had tried to buy that meal in Topeka.

Supreme Court Justice Joseph Bradley handed down the majority decision of eight of the nine judges. All were either Northerners or Westerners. All but Justice Stephen J. Field were Republicans and had supported Abraham Lincoln and the Union in the Civil War.

The eight judges said that the Civil Rights Act of 1875 was unconstitutional. Therefore the United States government could not and would not protect Bird Gee and other black people from racial discrimination in public facilities.

The Fourteenth Amendment, said Justice Bradley, protects an individual's rights and liberties against any act of the state he happens to be in. In the case of Bird Gee the amendment would protect him from racial discrimination by the state of Kansas or the city of Topeka.

But Murray Stanley was a private individual. And in refusing to serve Gee he was acting as a private individual. Such was the situation in all the other civil-right cases. Davis, Agee, Tyler, and Mrs. Robinson were all discriminated against by individuals, not by states or cities.

"Individual invasion of individual rights," wrote Bradley, "is not the subject matter of the Amendment." Therefore, he said, echoing *United States v. Cruikshank,* Congress had no authority to pass a law prohibiting racial discrimination by private citizens.

Justice Bradley said more. He said that the purpose of the Fourteenth Amendment and the other Civil War amendments had been to help the newly freed Negro. But now things had gone too far. Blacks were getting too much help. There was a limit. And Justice Bradley was going to set that limit by seeing that the Negro stopped being "the special favorite of the laws."

Justice Bradley also argued that the rights protected by the Civil Rights Act were what he called "social" rights. But the Fourteenth Amendment was concerned solely with legal rights. For this reason too, therefore, the Civil Rights Act of 1875 was unconstitutional.

One eloquent voice disagreed with the Supreme Court majority. It was the voice of the Court's only Southerner—a former slaveowner from Kentucky, Justice John Marshall Harlan.

John Marshall Harlan was the only member of the Supreme Court to rule that the Civil Rights Act of 1875 was constitutional. Justice Harlan, a former slave owner and the only Southerner on the Court, was one of the few prominent white Americans to support black rights.

But most white Americans agreed with Bradley. The New York *Times,* Chicago *Tribune,* and Washington *Post* thought it a wise decision. White people in Atlanta, Georgia, celebrated. The Supreme Court had given them the go-ahead signal to discriminate against Negroes without fear of being arrested and punished.

In the national capital, Frederick Douglass wrote bitterly that Southern racists could now do what they pleased with the Negro. "They can put him in a smoking car or baggage car . . . take him or leave him at a railroad station, exclude him from all places of amusement or instruction, without the least fear that the national government will interfere for the protection of his liberty."

In this way the Supreme Court deleted the Civil Rights Act of 1875 from the law books.

In 1883 there wasn't any pressure from the American public to enforce the Fourteenth Amendment. The black minority was weak. The white majority was indifferent or hostile. Americans were more interested in the new business corporations that were then building factories, railroads, and mining towns all across America.

The Supreme Court, which represented the white majority, reflected that attitude. Although the Court may not "follow the election returns," as some people claim, it is influenced by public opinion.

While the Court was deciding that the Fourteenth Amendment did not protect blacks like Bird Gee or Sallie Robinson, the Court said that the amendment *did* protect business corporations! The Court did this by deciding that business corporations were "persons." State laws regulating the activities of corporations denied them—according to the Supreme Court—the "equal protection of the laws" guaranteed to "all persons" by the Fourteenth Amendment.

The clearest statement of this concern for the rights of corporations came in the case of *Santa Clara County v. Southern Pacific Railroad* in 1886. In his ruling in this case Chief Justice Morrison R. Waite said:

> The Court does not wish to hear argument on the question whether the provision in the Fourteenth Amendment to the Constitution, which forbids a State to deny to any person within its jurisdiction the equal protection of the laws, applies to these corporations. We are all of the opinion that it does.

Under this interpretation the Supreme Court declared unconstitutional many state laws attempting to regulate business corporations—laws requiring employers to protect the safety of their workers, laws limiting the labor of children and women, and laws requiring employers to pay decent wages. From the 1880s well into the twentieth century the Court said, in effect, that no state could pass and enforce any law requiring a corporation to spend its money on behalf of its workers or of the community. In these years, four out of every five Supreme Court cases involving the "equal protection" clause of the Fourteenth Amendment were cases concerning the "equal protection" of business corporations.

Bird Gee, Sallie Robinson, and the millions of other black Americans who thought the Fourteenth Amendment was *their* shield of liberty were learning a bitter lesson.

By 1892, encouraged by the Court's decision in the *Civil Rights Cases,* nine Southern states had passed laws requiring—not just permitting—railroads to carry black passengers in separate cars (known as "Jim Crow" cars) or behind partitions. One of these states was Louisiana.

Blacks in Louisiana decided to test the Separate Car Law. Backed by the militant black newspaper *Crusader,* the Citizens Committee to Test the Constitutionality of the Separate Car Law began to collect money for the case.

On June 7, 1892, the test began. Homer Adolph Plessy, a light-colored black, bought a ticket in New Orleans for Covington, Louisiana. He got on the train and took a seat in the "white" car. When the conductor asked Plessy to move to the Jim Crow car, he refused. The train was held at the station until the police came and arrested Plessy.

His lawyer was Albion Tourgée, a white Northerner who had been a Radical Republican in North Carolina during Reconstruction days. Tourgée argued before a New Orleans judge, John B. Ferguson, that the Jim Crow state law was unconstitutional because it violated the Fourteenth Amendment—which forbade any state law depriving a citizen of his equal rights. Judge Ferguson ruled against him and declared Plessy guilty of violating the state law. Tourgée then appealed the case of *Plessy v. Ferguson* through the Louisiana state courts to the Supreme Court of the United States.

Tourgée made the same point in his argument before the Supreme Court in Washington that he had made before Judge Ferguson in New Orleans. He said:

> The object of such a law is simply to debase and distinguish against the inferior race. Its purpose has been properly interpreted by the general designation of "Jim Crow Car" law. Its object is to separate the Negroes from the whites in public conveyances for the gratification and recognition of the sentiment of white superiority and white supremacy.

Tourgée raised another legal point. What right did the state have "to label one citizen as white and another as colored"? "The law," he argued, "ought at least to be color-blind."

It took more than three years for the Supreme Court to announce a decision in the case of *Plessy v. Ferguson.*

And then on May 18, 1896, the Supreme Court handed down its answer. Justice Henry Brown, a Michigan Republican born in Massachusetts, gave the opinion of the majority.

They approved of racial segregation. They said that a state *did* have the right to label its citizens according to race and to enforce their separation in public facilities.

Jim Crow was now not only legal and official; it could also be made compulsory.

Justice Brown added that he did not think that state-enforced racial segregation made black people "unequal." White people, he said, were separated too. If such laws made black people seem unequal, he said, "it is solely because the colored race chooses to put that construction upon it."

Justice Brown and the six other judges for whom he spoke must have been the only men in the United States who did not think that racial segregation was designed to degrade black people. White Southerners openly boasted that the degradation of Negroes was the sole purpose of the Jim Crow laws. Justice Brown was accepting the tricky language of the Louisiana law—"equal but separate accommodations"—to get around the purpose of the Fourteenth Amendment.

Nobody—that is, no white people—paid much attention to the *Plessy v. Ferguson* decision. The New York *Times* reported it on May 19 in its "News of the Railroad" department in the back of the paper— down near the bottom of the page. Up at the top of the column, the most prominent news story concerned a report from the U.S. Department of Agriculture about the proper way to treat cattle as they were shipped by railroad from one part of the country to another.

Justice John Marshall Harlan, however, did have

something to say. He scorned the majority's argument that segregation did not discriminate against Negroes. "Everyone knows," he said, that the purpose of Jim Crow laws is "to exclude colored people from coaches occupied by or assigned to white persons." He agreed with lawyer Tourgée that the purpose of such laws was to create a system of white supremacy and black inferiority.

"But in view of the Constitution," Harlan protested, "there is in this country no superior, dominant ruling class of citizens." And he added: "Our constitution is color-blind."

The *Plessy v. Ferguson* decision appeared to mark the death of the Fourteenth Amendment. Thirty years after the amendment had been passed by Congress, equal rights for black Americans had no support in law. In the 1896 decision, the Court said simply and brutally: *Negroes may not be slaves any more, but they are not free citizens either. This Court will not support their right to equality with white people.*

Thirty-seven years before Nazi Germany passed laws classifying Germans by "race," the Supreme Court had approved racial laws in the United States.

The Triumph of Jim Crow

Southern states—and even some cities and towns in states that were not Southern—eagerly followed the path pointed out by the Supreme Court. From 1896 on, black Americans were fair game for racists and racist laws.

Signs saying "white only" or "colored" began to sprout. Toilets, drinking fountains, waiting rooms, ticket windows—almost every conceivable place and facility—were carefully labeled by race to make sure that white and black people did not meet on terms of equality. Most of these Jim Crow rules were local or state laws and were enforced by the police.

Others were enforced just as effectively as if they were law. The police arrested a black man if he tried to use a facility labeled "white" even if the labeling was not supported by a Jim Crow law. The police called his "crime" disorderly conduct or disturbing the peace.

Oklahoma passed a law requiring separate telephone booths for blacks and whites. North Carolina and Florida segregated their public-school textbooks, so that white children would not have to use the same books black children used. In Florida, the textbooks were segregated even while in storage. In South Carolina, black factory workers were forbidden to "use" the same windows as white workers.

Courts of justice segregated black and white spectators and witnesses. In some Georgia courtrooms, black witnesses had to swear on a different Bible from that used by whites. In some buildings there were separate elevators for blacks and whites. Prisons, hospitals, schools, and other public facilities were rigidly segregated.

Ambulances for "white" hospitals refused to carry black patients. "White" hospitals refused to treat them. An uncounted number of black accident victims died because they were denied help by "white" ambulances, hospitals, or doctors. The famous blues singer Bessie Smith died in 1937 because a "white" hospital in Mississippi refused to treat her injuries.

Dr. Charles R. Drew, whose research on blood plasma led to the development of blood banks, was another victim of hospital segregation. Seriously injured in an automobile accident in North Carolina, he was not treated at the nearest hospital—because it was "white." On his way to the "colored" hospital farther away, the inventor of the blood bank bled to death.

Public libraries would not allow black taxpayers to borrow books or even to take out library cards. Some libraries would permit a black person to borrow a book only if that person brought a note from a white

Dr. Charles Drew, head of the American Red Cross blood banks in World War II, was a victim of medical Jim Crow.

person. The idea of allowing black people to read books or educate themselves was not popular in the South. White people preferred to keep black people as ignorant as possible, so that most of them would remain farm workers, housemaids, and unskilled factory workers and porters.

Some black Southern professors could not even use the public libraries where their own books were on the shelves.

The Supreme Court's decision in *Plessy v. Ferguson* enabled the South to draw the color line through all walks of life. Where black and white Americans had ridden the railroads together in peace and equality, after 1896 black people had to ride separately. In buses and streetcars they had to sit in the back. If a white person was standing, a black person who was seated had to give up his or her seat. It made no difference if the black person was old, or sick, or a woman carrying a baby.

In all aspects of life, even in the pettiest details, the color line was there to separate black from white. Some states barred black people from their public parks. Some park benches were labeled "white only." Swimming pools and beaches were segregated. In department stores, black customers were not allowed to try clothes on.

Justice Harlan must have shaken his head in amazement and horror at how much he had underestimated the effects of the *Plessy v. Ferguson* decision. In his dissenting opinion, he had predicted, half sarcastically, that if a state could enforce racial segregation on its railroads it might someday do the same in its juries, courtrooms, and other public places. Now the Southern states were going far beyond his predictions in humiliating and degrading their black residents.

Not a soul believed the words of Justice Brown that segregation was "equal" for black and white. No one believed the phrase "separate but equal." Everyone knew that the purpose of the Jim Crow laws was to teach black people their "place." Everyone, black and white, knew where that place was: beneath the "superior" white race.

If there was any possibility of doubt, the very nature of the segregated facilities proved their inequality. "Black" facilities were almost always smaller, dirtier, more inconvenient, harder to get to. In many cases there were no "black" facilities at all, and blacks were just excluded from the one "white" facility. This was especially the case with swimming pools, libraries, and parks. In some cases, Jim Crow laws

The Supreme Court, in the case of Plessy v. Ferguson, *said that "separate but equal" was constitutional. Most public facilities, however, turned out to be separate but unequal.*

even required that the sign saying "white" had to be bigger and handsomer than the one saying "colored." Ten years after *Plessy v. Ferguson* the Supreme Court ruled that a state could force white people to discriminate against black people even if they did not want to. In Kentucky, Berea College had taught black and white students together since the Civil War. But in 1904 the state of Kentucky passed a law forbidding the teaching of black and white students in the same school. The state fined Berea College $1,000 for violation of this law. The college appealed to the Supreme Court.

The Court ruled that Kentucky was within its rights and that Berea College had to obey the Jim Crow law. Once more, the only dissenting voice was that of Justice Harlan. "Have we become so inoculated with prejudice of race?" he asked.

The answer was "yes." Sadly, Berea College said good-by to its black students. The white students sent a farewell letter to their classmates. "Our sense of justice shows us that others have the same rights as ourselves," it said. "We hope never to be afraid or ashamed to show our approval of any colored person."

Again the states and cities of the South rushed to follow the Court's lead. They passed laws making it a crime for white people to associate voluntarily with black people. Where black and white citizens were allowed to meet together, laws provided that they must sit separately, eat separately, use separate washrooms, and enter and leave by different doors. In countless cases in the South the sight of a white or black family entertaining visitors of the other race resulted in a call for the police and a threatened arrest.

Supreme Court Justice David J. Brewer, a nephew of Justice Stephen J. Field, put the Court's attitude in a single eloquent sentence. An Arkansas Negro appealed to the Court for protection from a white lynch mob. The Court said, in Justice Brewer's words, that blacks "will have to take their chances with other citizens in the states where they make their homes."

In that same year, 1905, more than a hundred black Americans were burned at the stake, tortured, and murdered by white lynch mobs in the states where they made their homes.

Black Americans fell back in defeat. They saw the bright hopes of Reconstruction gone. Under the thumb of the white South, abandoned by the white North, they tried to find some way out of their dilemma. They were a minority of less than 8 million, surrounded by 67 million whites. They had few votes, little wealth, no political power. They were ignored by Congress, by the President, and by the Supreme Court. Only the lonely, ineffectual voice of Justice John Marshall Harlan was raised in their behalf.

These black Americans learned a bitter lesson: that for a weak minority the Constitution did not exist. The 90 percent of America that was white could ignore the rights of blacks, could violate the Fourteenth Amendment—and nothing would be done about it. Black people could be murdered, cheated, and abused; the law did not protect them. "Law and order" meant nothing to the white majority. *White America openly violated the Constitution.* Southern states deliberately and systematically found ways to keep black men from voting, in direct violation of the law. One part of the Fourteenth Amendment provided that if a state deprived any of its male citizens over 21 of the right to vote, that state would itself be deprived of a proportional number of Congressmen in the House of Representatives.

But that part of the Fourteenth Amendment, as we have seen, was never enforced, even though many black citizens were prevented from voting in several Southern states.

In their defeat, black people suffered severe economic hardship. Almost all of them lived in the South where many of them were servants or poor farm workers. A large number of them did not have enough to eat or decent clothing to wear. They were not able to educate their children. Black clergymen, teachers, and merchants suffered, too. Blacks who stood up for their rights risked a horrible death by lynching.

Under the circumstances, the right to ride a railroad train, or to use a waiting room, a drinking fountain, or a park bench, did not seem too important. When a prominent black man named Booker T. Washington said this in a public speech in Atlanta, he echoed the defeated spirit of many other black people. And he said what white people wanted to hear a black man say—that jobs and job training are more important than equal rights or an equal education.

Booker T. Washington was the head of Tuskegee Institute when he made his famous speech at Atlanta less than a year before the *Plessy v. Ferguson* decision. (It was the same year in which Frederick Douglass died.) White newspaper editors, preachers, and politicians applauded Washington and proclaimed him "leader of his people."

Overnight he became the most important and powerful black man in America, the white-appointed spokesman for his race. The President of the United States invited him to visit the White House.

Washington said that black Americans should forget about higher education, political rights, or equality. They should concentrate on being good workers: good farm workers and good factory workers. They

Booker T. Washington.

should not try to compete with white men.

He used language that sounded very much like the "separate but equal" doctrine that the Supreme Court thought justified Jim Crow laws. "In all things that are purely social," Washington said of the two races, "we can be as separate as the fingers, yet one as the hand in all things essential to mutual progress." And he added: "The opportunity to earn a dollar in a factory just now is worth infinitely more than the opportunity to spend a dollar in an opera house."

By no means all black Americans agreed with Washington. Many educated and intelligent black men were bitterly opposed to what they saw as a kind of "Uncle Tomism." Bishop Henry M. Turner of Atlanta delivered a speech just three months later in which he said:

> The colored man who will stand up and in one breath say that the [Negro] race does not want social equality and in the next predict a great future . . . is either an ignoramus or an advocate of the perpetual servility and degradation of his race.

Two months after that, the president of Atlanta University attacked Washington in these words:

> If we are not striving for equality, in heaven's name for what are we living? I regard it as cowardly and dishonest for any of our colored men to tell white people or colored people that we are not struggling for equality.

Booker T. Washington thought blacks ought to accept second-class citizenship in return for help from rich white men. And rich white men like Andrew Carnegie and John D. Rockefeller gave him millions and millions of dollars to provide schools and jobs for Southern black people.

Booker T. Washington believed that the only way the black man could get a foot on the ladder of advancement was to make himself useful to the white men who ruled the South. Washington was clever, cautious, and practical. He was not a liberation leader. But in his own way he thought he could lead blacks to equality by indirect roads.

He did not deceive himself about the decency and good will of even the rich whites who gave him money. "When your head is in the lion's mouth," he told fellow blacks, "use your hand to pet him." He was a general of retreat and compromise.

The retreat continued. In 1901 the last black Congressman from the South, George H. White of North Carolina, stood up on the floor of the House of Representatives and said good-by. "This, Mr. Chairman, is the Negro's temporary farewell to the American Congress. He will rise up some day and come again."

Lynch murders spread, and not only in the South. In 1908 Springfield, Illinois, the home city and resting place of Abraham Lincoln, was taken over by a white mob. The mob killed and wounded scores of blacks and burned down Negroes' homes. "Lincoln freed you," some of the mob shouted to the terrified black people. "We'll show you where you belong!"

In the early years of this century, between 100 and 150 black Americans were murdered annually by white mobs. Between 1900 and 1930 almost two thousand black people were tortured and murdered by lynch gangs. Often Southern policemen and sheriffs cooperated in these murders. Meanwhile Congress refused to pass a law making lynching a crime.

In 1913 the first Southern President to be elected since before the Civil War moved into the White House. His name was Woodrow Wilson. He was a Democrat, a college president, and a liberal. Under his administration, orders were issued requiring segregated rest rooms and lunchrooms for federal employees. Until 1913 black and white employees of the Treasury, Post Office, and other departments had used these facilities together. Now, under Woodrow Wilson, Jim Crow came to the federal government itself.

Black Americans realized that they could not depend on the good will of the white majority. And they could not depend on the promise of the Fourteenth Amendment, a promise now more than half a century old and still unfulfilled.

Yet it *was* a promise. The words were there in the Constitution. Somehow, in some way, they would have to be brought to life and enforced. But that would not happen by itself. Nor would it happen because of the conscience of white America. There were very few John Marshall Harlans.

Black men would have to see to it themselves that the Fourteenth Amendment was enforced.

A New Leadership for Blacks

When Booker T. Washington made his famous speech in Atlanta, William E. B. Du Bois was 27 years old. He had been born in Great Barrington, Massachusetts, the year the Fourteenth Amendment was ratified. The Du Bois family were free people. None of them had been slaves for almost a hundred years before William was born.

In 1895, when Washington was telling black people they ought to be satisfied with the right to earn a dollar as unskilled farmers or factory workers, Du Bois was getting his Ph.D. degree at Harvard. He was the first black man to earn a doctorate at Harvard. After that he became a professor at Atlanta University.

Not many Americans—white or black—went to college in the 1890s. Fewer still went to Harvard. Ph.D.s were rare indeed. Du Bois was an unusual man.

But he was not the only black American who was going to college in those days. In the year 1900 there were 2500 black college graduates in the United States. When President Woodrow Wilson forced black government workers to use Jim Crow rest rooms and Jim Crow lunchrooms, there were about 40,000 Negro businesses in the United States. Many black businessmen, as well as many black professional men and women, became militant fighters for the rights of Afro-Americans.

There was William Monroe Trotter, editor and publisher of the Boston *Guardian.* Trotter's first editorial in the *Guardian* was an attack on Booker T. Washington as a traitor to his race. And Trotter had protested to Woodrow Wilson in person when the President extended segregation in the federal service.

There was Ida Wells Barnett, born in Mississippi just after the Civil War. She was a schoolteacher in Memphis, Tennessee, before she became editor and owner of the Memphis *Free Speech.* When her paper exposed a white lynch mob in 1892, the hoodlums burned her house and drove her out of the state. Ida Wells Barnett published a study of lynching, *A Red Record,* which was the first statistical analysis of this crime against black people.

All through the first and second decades of the twentieth century, a growing number of black doctors, lawyers, teachers, and preachers felt that it was time to carry out the Fourteenth Amendment's promise—equal protection of the laws. They did not believe that black Americans should accept second-class citizenship. They did not want to ask rich white men for charity.

These black activists found their spokesmen in young Professor Du Bois. Du Bois believed that black

William E. B. Du Bois wanted the Fourteenth Amendment to be carried out. He stated the goal of early black militants in nine words: "The enforcement of the Constitution of the United States."

people should strive to be more than servants or farm laborers. He wanted black boys and girls to try to educate themselves to be doctors, lawyers, scientists, and teachers. He wanted them to work for the benefit of their fellow Afro-Americans.

In 1904 Washington and Du Bois tried to work out their differences. They did not succeed. Du Bois and his friends went on to develop a new leadership for black people. No longer would whites be able to point to Booker T. Washington as the sole "leader of his people."

To show the world what he thought, Du Bois wrote his *Credo* (Latin for "I Believe"). It was published widely in 1904 in black newspapers. Hundreds of black families framed it and hung it in their homes. *Credo* said in part:

> I believe that all men, black and brown and white, are brothers. . . .
> I believe in the Negro Race; in the beauty of its genius, the sweetness of its soul. . . .
> I believe in pride of race and lineage itself; in pride of self so deep as to scorn injustice to other selves. . . .
> I believe in liberty for all men; the space to stretch their arms and their souls; the right to breathe and the right to vote, the freedom to choose their friends, enjoy the sunshine and ride on the railroads, uncursed by color.

A year later Du Bois sent out a letter to black leaders throughout the country. He called upon them to come together to form a new organization to fight for Negro rights.

The summer of 1905, 29 young black men from 14 states met in Canada, just across the border from Buffalo, New York. They met in Canada because the hotel on the American side would not rent them rooms. They called themselves the Niagara Movement, after nearby Niagara Falls. They agreed to fight for Negro rights and to reject the advice of Booker T. Washington.

The next summer they met again, at Harpers Ferry in West Virginia. This time there were a hundred people present. Some were women, some were white. At dawn on August 18, someone read aloud the words of the Niagara *Address to the Country*, written by Dr. W. E. B. Du Bois:

> We claim for ourselves every single right that belongs to a freeborn American. . . . Until we get these rights we will never cease to protest. . . .
> We want full manhood suffrage and we want it now. . . .
> We want discrimination in public accommodation to cease. . . .
> We want the Constitution of the country enforced. . . . We want the Fourteenth Amendment carried out to the letter, and every State disfranchised in Congress which attempts to disfranchise its rightful voters.

The *Address to the Country* closed with fighting words that drew a sharp line of disagreement with Booker T. Washington:

> We refuse to surrender the leadership of this race to cowards. . . . We are men; we will be treated as men. . . . We shall never give up. . . .
> And we shall win.

The experience of the Niagara Movement contributed to the birth of the National Association for the Advancement of Colored People (NAACP). Three years after the Harpers Ferry meeting, the NAACP was born. Among its charter members were Du Bois and Ida Wells Barnett.

The NAACP began a series of lawsuits aimed at enforcing the Fourteenth Amendment. One of these concerned Jim Crow housing in the Kentucky city of

Louisville. Louisville had passed an ordinance forbidding blacks and whites to live on the same block. Even though the Fourteenth Amendment had been weakened by Supreme Court decisions, it was still part of the Constitution. The Court and Southern lawmakers might twist and distort its language. They might get around its provisions. But they could not ignore it entirely.

The phrase "equal but separate" had been put in the Louisiana Separate Car Law to make it look as if the law did not violate the "equal protection" words of the Fourteenth Amendment. The Supreme Court had accepted this evasion in *Plessy v. Ferguson*.

The Louisville housing law was also worded cleverly. According to the law, it was illegal for a white man to sell his house to a Negro, or for a Negro to sell his house to a white man. That sounded "equal." And the law said its purpose was "to prevent conflict and ill-feeling between the white and colored races . . . by . . . requiring . . . the use of separate blocks for residence."

In 1917, when the NAACP took the matter to the Supreme Court in the case of *Buchanan v. Warley,* things were changing. For one thing, the country was now in the midst of the first World War. The United States, said President Wilson, was fighting "to make the world safe for democracy."

For many sensitive Americans it was time to make America a little more democratic at home. Two hundred thousand black Americans were serving overseas in the armed forces, a quarter of them in combat

For bravery in action in World War I, these black Americans received the French government's Croix de Guerre medal.

units. They were fighting to save democracy, according to Woodrow Wilson. Yet they could not enjoy democracy at home.

Black people were moving north, out of the rural South into the cities of Philadelphia, Chicago, and New York. They were taking jobs in the factories that were busy making war materials.

These black migrants got the lowest-paid jobs. They had to live in the worst slums. They met racial discrimination in the North, too.

But they were out from under the whip and the gun

of Southern sheriffs. They had a little more freedom to organize and to fight for their rights. They could protest. They began to vote. Some of them were able to educate themselves or their children. They could listen to black newspapermen like Monroe Trotter. They could support the new NAACP and could read its monthly magazine, *Crisis,* edited by W. E. B. Du Bois.

And perhaps by 1917 the Supreme Court was a bit more sensitive to black rights. Justice Harlan had been dead for six years. But if he had been alive, he would have found himself this time voting with the majority. For in 1917 the Court ruled unanimously, in *Buchanan v. Warley,* that the Louisville housing law was unconstitutional.

The law violated the Fourteenth Amendment, said the Court. It also violated the Civil Rights Act of 1866 which said in part:

> All citizens of the United States shall have the same right in every state and territory as is enjoyed by white citizens thereof to inherit, purchase, lease, sell, hold and convey real and personal property.

The Louisville law interfered with this right, said the Court, because it denied black people the right to sell their property as they wished. "Colored persons," wrote Justice William R. Day, "are citizens of the United States and have the right to purchase property and enjoy the use of same without laws discriminating against them solely on account of color."

Buchanan v. Warley was hardly a momentous case.

It did not mark an important turning point for black Americans. Jim Crow, supported by *Plessy v. Ferguson,* was still the law of the land. Other ways were found to accomplish segregation in housing and in big-city neighborhoods.

But the Supreme Court's unanimous decision against the Louisville housing law suggested that a turn was coming in American life.

The years following *Buchanan v. Warley* saw the rise of Harlem as the largest and most important black urban community in the whole world. By 1924 there were more black people living there than in any Southern city. Harlem became the Negro capital, a center of black art, black culture, and black politics.

Those were the years of the Negro Renaissance. Black poets, artists, writers, and entertainers flourished. White Americans began to discover the talents of black poets like Langston Hughes, Claude McKay, and Arna Bontemps. Marcus Garvey rose to fame with powerful black nationalist speeches and appeals for American blacks to return to Africa.

In 1930, thirteen years after *Buchanan v. Warley,* a Republican President nominated a Southern conservative judge to the Supreme Court. The President was Herbert Hoover. He had won election with strong Southern support, the first Republican ever to get such support. Hoover carried seven Southern states. And now he was paying for that support by nominating Judge John J. Parker of North Carolina to the Court.

Judge Parker had said publicly that he did not believe it would be good for the country to permit blacks to take part in politics. That remark alone would not disqualify him. There had been other racists on the Supreme Court.

But something happened this time. A President's appointment to the Supreme Court must be approved by the Senate. The NAACP, working hard to defeat Parker, told every Senator about his bigoted background.

Now, for the first time in the twentieth century, the Senate refused to approve a President's choice for the Supreme Court. Northern Republicans deserted their party and voted against him. By a vote of 41 to 39 the nomination was defeated. It was a victory for black people and their friends, a defeat for racists.

In 1930 racial prejudice was losing some of its popularity. The climate of opinion in the United States was changing, even if only slightly. White Americans might still be racist, but they were not boasting about it quite so openly.

The 1930s were years of hardship for all Americans. The Great Depression threw millions of people out of work. The country was desperate. People were beginning to question and criticize the old way of doing things.

The labor unions began to change. Under the old American Federation of Labor the unions took in only skilled workers, and often these unions were for whites only. (Today black workers are still kept from full participation in some union programs and even denied membership in some unions.) But by the 1930s many black workers had come north to take unskilled and semi-skilled jobs. They worked in the steel mills, the rubber plants, the automobile factories, and the coal mines. When the Depression came and the mills and factories closed their doors, black and white men found themselves in the same boat—jobless.

The new Congress of Industrial Organizations (CIO), led by John L. Lewis of the miners' union, set out to organize these factory workers into giant unions. To do this they had to appeal to both black and white workers.

Now, for the first time, racism came to be seen as a danger to white people. Hatred of Negroes would divide the workers against each other and keep them from building strong unions. Under a new slogan, "Black and white unite and fight," hundreds of thousands of workers were organized into new CIO unions all over the country.

The unity of black and white workers in the labor movement had a profound influence on the nation. Millions of Americans, including young students who had never been inside a factory, came to see racism as an enemy of America. Hating black people came to be seen as not only immoral and undemocratic but also anti-labor.

At the same time, Americans in the 1930s could see how the German people lost their freedom when they allowed their leaders to blind them with anti-Jewish racism. At home the supporters of President Franklin D. Roosevelt's New Deal began to look upon anti-black racism with suspicion. A whole generation of young white Americans began to ally themselves with the struggles of their black fellow Americans. And they became critical of American institutions that had permitted racism to flourish.

The Supreme Court came in for a good deal of this criticism. The Court seemed to stand in the way of progress. Its members were still conservative at a time when the mood of many Americans was increasingly radical. When the Court justices opposed President Roosevelt's plans to get the country back on its feet again, he ridiculed them as "nine old men."

The Court may have been on the defensive when it handed down its two decisions in the Scottsboro case in the 1930s.

The "Scottsboro boys" were nine blacks, aged 13 to 19, who had been falsely accused of raping two white girls. The trial was held in the small rural town of Scottsboro, Alabama. The young men were tried, convicted, and sentenced to death—all but the youngest one. During the trial the town and the courthouse were surrounded by a mob of thousands of shouting white men who threatened to lynch the blacks if they were set free.

The Scottsboro boys attracted the attention of white sympathizers in the North and in foreign countries. Great meetings were held to protest the death penalty. Books and plays were written about the case. Radical groups, Communists and Socialists,

Heywood Patterson, one of the nine Scottsboro defendants, on the witness stand. Although the death sentences were not carried out, the young men served long years in prison.

raised money and sent lawyers to help them. The NAACP provided legal aid. In Europe, crowds demonstrated in front of U.S. embassies calling for the freedom of the Scottsboro boys.

The Supreme Court ruled in 1932, in the case of *Powell v. Alabama,* that the Scottsboro boys had not had a fair trial because they had been denied proper legal advice. The Court also ruled that the defendants had not been allowed enough time to prepare their defense.

In 1935, in the case of *Norris v. Alabama,* the Court found that the jury which convicted the Scottsboro boys had been chosen from a panel that excluded blacks. This, said the Court, deprived the defendants of the equal protection of the laws guaranteed by the Fourteenth Amendment.

In the Scottsboro decisions, for the first time since Reconstruction, the Supreme Court acted effectively to protect the rights of blacks to receive a fair trial in the South. And the Court based its reasoning on the Fourteenth Amendment.

The NAACP Campaigns for the Fourteenth Amendment

On the eve of the second World War, while white Americans worried about threats to democracy in Europe, black Americans still suffered under racial laws at home.

Black Americans remained second-class citizens, forced to ride Jim Crow cars and use Jim Crow toilets. Schools in the South (and some in the North) segregated blacks. Restaurants refused to serve them, or forced them to sit separately. Hotels in Washington within sight of the White House and the Capitol refused to accept them as guests. Tricky new laws kept them from voting in Southern states.

The second World War came, another "war for democracy." More than a million black men marched off to fight for American freedom—marched in a Jim Crow army.

Most black soldiers were put in construction and transportation units. Few black units were permitted to carry guns into combat. Most blacks who were armed were kept away from battle—for fear that they

CITY CAFE

COLORED ENTRANCE

might show the world they were as brave as white men.

On Army bases, black soldiers lived in separate, crowded, inferior barracks. They were not allowed to use PX stores with white soldiers. In the South, when they went into town, they had to put up with abuses and insults from local white policemen and sheriffs. Some black servicemen were murdered by Southern policemen. Their uniform did not protect them.

When captured Nazi soldiers were brought back to prison camps in the United States, they were allowed to eat their meals in railroad dining cars as they rolled through the South. But the dining cars would not serve black Americans. So the black military policemen who often guarded the prisoners had to dine on candy bars on dusty open railroad platforms. In Southern states prisoners of war were served in restaurants, while black soldiers had to go around to the back to eat in the kitchen.

But change was in the air. Black men continued to

rebel. Overseas some black soldiers fought pitched battles with white soldiers who abused them. Some fought back with arms against Southern policemen who attacked them. After the war, returning black veterans marched to courthouses in the South and demanded the right to vote. Many white Americans, revolted at Nazi racism and the concentration-camp atrocities, could no longer stomach American racism at home. They supported black demands for equal treatment.

One man who would not let Jim Crow hold him back was Heman Marion Sweatt of Houston, Texas. Sweatt was a slim, bespectacled man of 33. He was a letter carrier in Houston, and he wanted to become a lawyer.

Sweatt had graduated from a small "black" college in Texas. He had finished two years of graduate school at the University of Michigan. Now, in 1945, he applied to the public university of his home state, the University of Texas Law School.

Under the Texas constitution, black and white students could not go to school together. The University of Texas Law School was "white." Sweatt was the first black man to apply for admission. He was refused.

That might have been the end of the matter—except for the NAACP.

Back in its early days a suspicious government agent once questioned W. E. B. Du Bois about the NAACP. "What is the aim of your organization?" asked the agent.

Du Bois answered: "The enforcement of the Constitution of the United States."

During the 1930s the NAACP stepped up its campaign to enforce the Constitution. It set up a legal department to fight cases of racial discrimination through the courts. The NAACP legal office became a kind of "war department" in the battle to enforce the Constitution—and in particular the Fourteenth Amendment.

In the same decade, President Franklin D. Roosevelt appointed liberal justices to the Supreme Court. After more than 50 years of protecting the civil rights of large corporations, the Court was becoming more concerned about the civil rights of individuals. Beginning with the Scottsboro cases the Court showed a new sympathy for Negro rights.

The NAACP hoped to bring before the Supreme Court as many challenges to Jim Crow as it could find. Under the leadership of Walter White, executive secretary of the NAACP, its legal department grew. Faculty members from Washington's Howard University helped to plan the campaign. They included Charles Houston, William Hastie, and Ralph Bunche. In 1938 a young black lawyer who had been educated at Howard joined the NAACP staff. His name was Thurgood Marshall.

He soon became the director of the campaign against Jim Crow. He argued case after case before the Supreme Court.

In 1945 Thurgood Marshall and his staff took up the case of Heman Sweatt versus the University of

Texas. (The case was officially known as *Sweatt v. Painter.*)

In an earlier case the Supreme Court had ruled that blacks must be admitted to "white" schools unless "equal facilities" were provided by the state. But Texas had no other law school. Marshall therefore argued that Sweatt must be admitted immediately.

When the lower courts delayed and delayed, Marshall appealed to a higher court, demanding not

Although Heman Sweatt had finished two years of graduate work, it took him five years and a Supreme Court decision to gain admission to the University of Texas Law School.

"equal facilities" but the total end of racial segregation. "The requirements of the Fourteenth Amendment," said the NAACP legal brief, "can only thus be met."

The Texas officials were frightened at this challenge to Jim Crow. "If we don't do something quickly," said one state senator, "the United States Supreme Court will rule that your child and my child will have to attend school with Negroes."

The panicky Texas legislators found two million dollars to start building a "Negro" law school. Meanwhile they set up, almost overnight, a temporary "Negro" school, in order to keep Sweatt from going to school with whites.

This makeshift law school had no full-time faculty, no full-time librarian, only a handful of law books, no law journal, no practice law courts—and only one student. It was situated in a basement.

The regular University of Texas Law School had a full-time faculty of 16, a library of 65,000 books, a law journal, and 850 students. That law school was "for whites only."

Sweatt refused to attend the Jim Crow law school. Attorney Marshall appealed to the Supreme Court of the United States in an attack on the Court's 1896 *Plessy v. Ferguson* doctrine of "separate but equal." A separate "black" law school, he argued, cannot possibly be equal to a "white" law school. As a lawyer Sweatt would have to deal with white lawyers and white judges and district attorneys. A Jim Crow legal education would not prepare him for that.

In 1950 the Supreme Court agreed unanimously with the NAACP. Sweatt's constitutional rights, said the Court, entitled him to a legal education "equivalent to that offered by the State to students of other races." The Court ordered the University of Texas to admit Sweatt, which it did.

But the Court still refused to declare that the *Plessy v. Ferguson* decision of 1896 violated the Fourteenth Amendment. The Court seemed to be saying that as long as a state provided "equal facilities" for education, it could still require blacks and whites to go to different schools. It seemed to be avoiding a direct conflict with the 1896 decision.

On that same day the Court handed down a ruling in another case. George W. McLaurin had been admitted to a classroom at the University of Oklahoma. But his classroom seat was surrounded by a railing with a sign saying "Reserved for Colored." He was given a special desk in the library, and he had to eat at a special table in the university cafeteria.

The Supreme Court ordered the University of Oklahoma to stop. The Court said that under the Fourteenth Amendment, McLaurin "must receive the same treatment at the hands of the state as students of other races." Forcing McLaurin to study under those special circumstances, said the Court, "deprives him of his personal and present right to the equal protection of the laws."

The Supreme Court had not declared *Plessy v. Ferguson* dead. But it had seriously weakened the idea of "separate but equal." In some cases, said the Court, *separate* could not possibly be *equal.* And the Court was beginning to apply the Fourteenth Amendment phrase, "equal protection of the laws," to cases involving the rights of black Americans.

The date of the Sweatt and McLaurin decisions was June 5, 1950. NAACP lawyers drew up plans for a major attack on *Plessy v. Ferguson.*

Before George McLaurin was admitted to a University of Oklahoma classroom, he had to sit outside the doorway.

The End of "Separate but Equal"

Eight-year-old Linda Brown lived only five blocks from school. But she had to travel 21 blocks—because she was a black girl, and the school in her neighborhood was for white children only. This was not in Mississippi or South Carolina but in Topeka, Kansas.

Oliver Brown didn't think his daughter was being treated with the equality the Fourteenth Amendment said was her right. He thought she was being discriminated against. Why should she not go to the same school as the white children?

Just about the time the Supreme Court ordered the University of Texas to admit Heman Sweatt, Oliver Brown sued the Topeka Board of Education. His lawyer argued that the school board was depriving Linda of her constitutional rights under the Fourteenth Amendment. The Kansas federal court disagreed. Since the "black" school building was as good as the "white" school building, said the court, Linda was being treated equally as far as the law was concerned.

86   The End of "Separate but Equal"

But the court did criticize the "separate but equal" rule. Said the court:

> Segregation of white and colored children in public schools has a detrimental effect upon the colored children. The impact is greater when it has the sanction of the law; for the policy of separating the races is usually interpreted as denoting the inferiority of the Negro group. A sense of inferiority affects the motivation of a child to learn. Segregation with the sanction of law, therefore, has a tendency to [retard] the educational and mental development of Negro children and to deprive them of some of the benefits they would receive in a racially integrated school system.

However, the Kansas federal court felt it had to obey the Supreme Court's 1896 ruling in *Plessy v. Ferguson*. The court said therefore that Kansas had a right to permit racial segregation in its schools.

Oliver Brown's lawyer took his case against the Board of Education of Topeka to the Supreme Court.

Meanwhile other black schoolchildren and their parents decided it was time to claim the right to equal protection of the laws—the right to go to the same school and be educated in the same way as white children.

In Washington, D.C., Spottswood Bolling tried to go to the new "white" high school and was turned away. The Board of Education told him to go to the Jim Crow high school. Bolling's parents went to court.

In Claymont, Delaware, Ethel Belton and seven

Fifteen-year-old Spottswood Bolling with neighbors.

other teenagers were refused admission to the "white" high school. Like Linda Brown, the eight youngsters had to take long bus rides to get to and from the Jim Crow school. Their parents went to court.

Dorothy Davis was an active rebel. She took part in a student strike against crowded conditions in the Jim Crow school she had to attend in Prince Edward County, Virginia. The "white" school had plenty of room, but not for Dorothy. Her parents went to court.

In Clarendon County, South Carolina, black parents had been battling the county school board for years, ever since 1947 when they asked for a school bus for black children. When the board turned them down, they went to the NAACP for help.

Now the South Carolina parents were asking for more than buses. They wanted an equal education for their children. They wanted better school buildings, as many books as white children had, a lunchroom and a gymnasium in each school, more teachers. Everything that was given to white schoolchildren, the black parents claimed as the right of black schoolchildren. Clarendon County turned them down. Whereupon the black parents went to court.

The NAACP's Thurgood Marshall went to Charleston to argue their case before the three-man federal court there. Clarendon County's schools for Negro children were inferior to those for whites, said Marshall. He asked the court to declare South Carolina's separate school laws unconstitutional. Such laws, said Marshall, violate the Fourteenth Amendment's guarantee of equal protection of the laws.

The federal court agreed that the county schools for black children were inferior. It gave the county six months to improve them. But the court also said that according to *Plessy v. Ferguson* segregation was legal. South Carolina had a perfect right to send black children to Jim Crow schools.

By this time Marshall and the other NAACP lawyers had decided to launch their all-out attack on *Plessy v. Ferguson's* concept of "separate but equal." It was not enough to fight for "equal" rights. The hated word "separate" would always stand in the way as a badge of Negro inequality. Even courts that agreed with the NAACP, like the federal court in Kansas, would feel compelled to obey the rule of *Plessy v. Ferguson.*

NAACP lawyers sat down with psychologists, educators, law-school professors, and historians to prepare for the attack. They put together all the arguments and all the evidence to prove that *separate* could not possibly be *equal;* to prove that segregation in education was a violation of the Fourteenth Amendment; to prove that when Congressmen passed the amendment back in 1866, they intended it to wipe out all forms of racial discrimination.

All the school cases were put together because they all raised the same legal question. Since Linda Brown's case happened to reach the Supreme Court first, the title for the school segregation cases became *Brown v. Board of Education of Topeka.* Thurgood Marshall and his team of civil-rights lawyers put their arguments before the Court.

On May 17, 1954, one day before the 58th anniversary of the *Plessy v. Ferguson* decision of 1896, lawyers from all over the country crowded into the Supreme Court building to hear the Court's decision. John Davis, white-haired and distinguished-looking, lawyer for the segregated schools of South Carolina, waited. Thurgood Marshall and the other NAACP lawyers waited. And down in Clarendon County—and in homes all across the country—black parents and their children waited.

All nine judges were in agreement. The unanimous opinion was read aloud by Chief Justice Earl Warren. Speaking of the Fourteenth Amendment, he said:

> We cannot turn back the clock to 1868 when the Amendment was adopted, or even to 1896 when

May 17, 1954: Attorneys Hayes, Marshall, and Nabrit standing on the steps of the Supreme Court after their historic victory.

Plessy v. Ferguson was written. We must consider public education in the light of its full development and its present place in American life throughout the nation. Only in this way can it be determined if segregation in public schools deprives these plaintiffs of the equal protection of the laws.

Justice Warren then posed the main question of the school cases:

Does segregation of children in public schools solely on the basis of race, even though the physical facilities and other "tangible" factors may be equal, deprive the children of the minority group of equal educational opportunities?

And he answered that question for the entire Court: "We believe that it does." He continued:

> We conclude that in the field of public education the doctrine of "separate but equal" has no place. Separate educational facilities are inherently unequal. Therefore we hold that the plaintiffs and others similarly situated for whom the actions have been brought are, by reason of the segregation complained of, deprived of the equal protection of the laws guaranteed by the Fourteenth Amendment.

If Thaddeus Stevens and John M. Harlan had been there in that courtroom that day, they would have cheered. But the NAACP lawyers who *were* there—Thurgood Marshall, George E. C. Hayes, James M. Nabrit, and others—celebrated for them. And so did millions of Americans who wanted an end to discrimination.

"Separate" was dead. "Equal" was alive and well and had a fighting chance once more.

Within a year the Supreme Court issued an order to all public-school systems in the United States. It was an order to abandon segregated schools and to allow black and white children to go to school together. How fast? "With all deliberate speed," said the Supreme Court.

Putting Teeth in the Right to Be Equal

To racists and to Southern politicians the Supreme Court decision was a fearful shock. Bigots screamed "Never!" Southern Congressmen signed a manifesto vowing defiance of the Court. An anti-Negro judge in Mississippi referred to May 17, 1954, as "Black Monday."

To black people, and to white people of good will, the decision was a pointer that showed the way the wind was blowing. Black activists did not wait for new court cases to arise. They decided to put their own teeth in the Fourteenth Amendment.

About eighteen months after *Brown v. Board of Education* a quiet middle-aged lady named Rosa Parks started a revolution in Montgomery, capital city of the state of Alabama. Mrs. Parks was a seamstress. She started her revolution after a hard day's work when she refused to give up her bus seat and move to the back. For that she was arrested, fingerprinted, and fined. Mrs. Parks had broken a Montgomery law forbidding black people to sit in "white" seats.

Mrs. Parks's arrest set off a bus boycott in Montgomery. The black people of the city refused to ride the buses—and the bus company began to lose money. A brilliant young Baptist minister, the Rev. Dr. Martin Luther King, Jr., became the leader of the boycott.

Dr. King was only 26 years old in 1955. He was minister of the Dexter Avenue Baptist Church and well known in Montgomery's black community. But the outside world had never heard of him.

Rosa Parks and Martin Luther King.

The night the boycott was organized, he spoke to a crowd of thousands gathered in his church. "We are tired," he said, "tired of being kicked about by the brutal feet of oppression. We have no alternative but to protest."

The non-violent civil-rights protest movement had been born. It had found its leader. To the shock and surprise of Montgomery whites, the black people of this small Southern city held their bus boycott together.

They were attacked and beaten and insulted. Some of them were fired from their jobs. Their white bosses tried to bribe them to ride the buses. The police arrested Dr. King. Someone bombed his home. But the movement went on. The people held firm. The bus company lost more money.

In May, 1956, the boycotters went into federal court and sued the city of Montgomery. In December, a little more than a year after Rosa Parks refused to move to the back of the bus, the Supreme Court ruled in their favor. Alabama's bus laws violated the Fourteenth Amendment of the Constitution. Therefore they were illegal. Blacks could sit anywhere they pleased.

The civil-rights protest movement now developed new tactics. Dr. King became a national and international figure. Black Southerners were more determined than ever to see to it that the Fourteenth Amendment was enforced. All the work could not be left to lawyers arguing politely in Washington.

On a chilly afternoon in February, 1960, four black

Black youths trying in February, 1960—for the first time—to buy soft drinks at a soda fountain in Portsmouth, Virginia. Meanwhile, white youths had no trouble being served.

college students went into Woolworth's store in Greensboro, North Carolina, and sat down at the lunch counter.

"We don't serve colored here," the waitress said.

She might well have used the same words and the same tone of voice that the waiter used back in 1875 when he refused to serve Bird Gee in that Kansas restaurant.

But the four teenagers did not get up to look for the U.S. District Attorney, as Bird Gee had done. During 85 years blacks had learned a lesson. The four students refused to move. They sat there until closing time. The next morning they were back. When time came for them to go to class, their places were taken by other black sit-inners.

In the next few days, blacks sat down at lunch counters all over Greensboro. The movement spread to other college towns in South Carolina, Tennessee, Georgia, and Florida. Within a month or two, black students were sitting down and demonstrating for their right to be served in every Southern state.

The protest against Jim Crow at lunch counters spread to department stores, swimming pools, libraries, art galleries, theaters, restaurants, churches. It spread to every public facility where blacks had been segregated and humiliated since the Supreme Court had pulled the teeth out of the Fourteenth Amendment back in 1883 and 1896. There were "wade-ins," "pray-ins," "stand-ins," "swim-ins," "buy-ins"—all kinds and varieties of peaceful but militant acts of disobedience.

When demonstrators were arrested for breaking Jim Crow laws or "disturbing the peace," Thurgood Marshall and other NAACP attorneys went into court to defend them. Eventually the Supreme Court ruled that state and local police could not enforce laws which deprived individuals of the equal protection of the laws guaranteed by the Fourteenth Amendment.

In 1961 the Congress of Racial Equality (CORE) organized the Freedom Rides. CORE was a Northern civil-rights organization with black and white members. The Freedom Riders rode buses, trains, and planes up and down and across the country. They used "white" seats, "white" waiting rooms, "white" lunch counters, and "white" rest rooms wherever they found them. Where they were stopped, they sat down and refused to move. In some places, as in Anniston, Alabama, they were badly beaten. In other places they were thrown into jail by Southern police. But they persisted.

The sit-inners and the Freedom Riders were successful. Private restaurant owners and other private proprietors gave up and stopped segregating. Near the end of 1961 the Interstate Commerce Commission forbade racial discrimination on interstate buses and railroads and in their stations and terminals. Federal courts freed demonstrators as soon as local courts jailed them.

Much of public opinion was with the demonstrators. Northern politicians got the message. Northern Republican leader Senator Everett Dirksen quoted Victor Hugo that "nothing is as powerful as an idea whose time has come." Lyndon Johnson of Texas, who became President after the assassination of President John Kennedy, quoted to all Americans the words of the civil-rights song, "We Shall Overcome."

A year after the Montgomery bus boycott, Congress passed its first civil-rights act since 1875. It wasn't a very strong law. But the law did make it somewhat easier for black Southerners to vote. Black voting strength was growing in the North, too, especially in Illinois, New York, California and Pennsylvania.

In 1963, on August 28, a quarter of a million black and white Americans went to Washington to demand "Freedom Now!" The first speaker at the meeting at the Lincoln Memorial was Martin Luther King. After his famous "I have a dream" speech, the crowd went home. But they brought forth a new mood throughout the nation.

The following year Congress passed the Civil Rights Act of 1964. This law forbade discrimination in all privately owned public accommodations including restaurants, theaters, motels, hotels, and cemeteries. It said almost exactly what Charles Sumner's Civil Rights Act had said. In some places its language was even the same as the law of 1875—which the Supreme Court declared unconstitutional in the *Civil Rights Cases* of 1883.

But now—a few months after its passage—the Supreme Court upheld the Civil Rights Act of 1964. Once again it was constitutional for Congress to pass laws enforcing the "equal protection" guarantee of the Fourteenth Amendment.

In 1965 Congress passed the Federal Voting Rights Act, outlawing local restrictions on the right to vote. An important part of this law authorized federal examiners to register black voters in places where local officials had refused to register them.

The following year, more than 10,000 black voters registered in Selma, Alabama. In the election two years earlier, only 335 of Selma's black citizens had been able to vote.

In a few short years the Supreme Court had reversed its earlier decisions. It overruled the *Civil Rights Cases* of 1883. It overruled *Plessy v. Ferguson*

A few of the thousands who took part in the Selma march of January 1965, urging Alabama blacks to register and vote. Four months later the President signed the Federal Voting Rights Act.

of 1896. It prohibited segregation in public transportation. It forbade racial discrimination in all public accommodations. John Marshall Harlan's opinions were now the law of the land—more than half a century after his death.

The Fourteenth Amendment had been brought back to life by the successful efforts of black Americans.

Everybody's Fourteenth Amendment

Clarence Earl Gideon sat down in his jail cell in Florida and wrote a letter to the Supreme Court of the United States. Gideon was serving five years in Raiford Penitentiary after being found guilty of the crime of attempted burglary of a poolroom.

He wrote the letter in pencil on lined paper. He made mistakes in spelling. He used some words incorrectly. Gideon, a man in his fifties, hadn't had much schooling. This was the fifth time he'd been in jail.

But he wrote intelligently about his problem. He told the Supreme Court that the state of Florida had violated his right to a fair trial. "The question is very simple," he wrote. "I requested the court to appoint me an attorney and the court refused."

This happened in the summer of 1961, while the Freedom Riders were challenging segregation on the buses and trains of the South. Talk about equal rights was in the air. Clarence Earl Gideon was white, not black. He had no interest in the civil-rights movement. But he must have heard enough about the struggle for equal rights to raise questions in his mind.

Clarence Earl Gideon told the Supreme Court in 1961 that his rights under the Fourteenth Amendment had been violated. In 1963 the Supreme Court agreed.

Was a poor man entitled to equality? Was he entitled to the same right to have a lawyer as a rich man—even if he couldn't afford to pay for one? Even if he was a criminal, a man who had spent more than half his adult life in jail?

The state of Florida said no and denied Gideon a lawyer. At his trial, Gideon had to act as his own attorney. He did a pretty good job, but not good enough. The jury found him guilty, and the judge put him in jail for five years. Gideon wrote to the supreme court of Florida asking for a new trial. The court turned him down. Now he was writing to the highest court in the land.

Gideon said his rights under the Fourteenth Amendment had been violated. He claimed that it was impossible for a man to have a fair trial if he did not have a lawyer. The Fourteenth Amendment said that a man couldn't be put in jail without "due process of law"—a phrase that seemed to guarantee a fair trial.

Just twenty years earlier, in the case of *Betts v. Brady,* the Supreme Court had said that the Fourteenth Amendment did *not* guarantee a poor man the right to a lawyer. But Gideon didn't know that.

Nor did he know that the Court had been slowly changing its mind since that time. All the cases brought to the Court by the NAACP had made the justices look a little harder at the Fourteenth Amendment. The struggles of black people for *their* equality had made many white Americans think about the Fourteenth Amendment's guarantee.

Gideon had written his letter at just the right time. Earlier that year, two of the Court's judges had said that denying a poor man the right to a lawyer was unfair and unequal treatment. A little while later one of the two, Justice William J. Brennan, Jr., said that denying legal counsel to a man because he couldn't afford to pay for it "seems . . . to be . . . a case of the violation of the guarantee of equal protection of the laws."

Justice Brennan referred to an earlier case when he said: "A state may violate the equal protection clause [of the Fourteenth Amendment] if it fails at its expense to provide a convicted [poor man] with a transcript of the trial proceedings."

A year and a half after Gideon wrote his long letter, the Supreme Court ruled unanimously that the state of Florida *had* violated the Fourteenth Amendment. A poor man accused of a crime, said the Court, has as much right to a lawyer as a rich man. If he cannot afford one, the state will have to provide one for him at public expense.

The state of Florida was ordered to give Gideon a new trial. It did so, this time appointing a lawyer to represent him. This time Gideon won. He walked out of court a free man.

It probably never occurred to him to call up Thurgood Marshall at the NAACP headquarters and say, "Thank you." But the struggle of black people to enforce the Fourteenth Amendment had helped to make it possible for the Court to order a second trial for Clarence Earl Gideon.

When black people claimed their equality they forced all Americans to think about what that word equality really meant. And when black people won some of their equality, they encouraged others to fight for theirs.

The times were changing. Opinion about the Fourteenth Amendment was changing, too. In the minds of men and women concerned with justice, it was becoming more than a Civil War amendment to protect the rights of former slaves. As shown in the case of Clarence Earl Gideon, the Fourteenth Amendment could protect the right of a poor man, accused of a crime, to a fair trial.

In 1963 the President received a report from his Commission on the Status of Women. The report urged that the Fourteenth Amendment be used to extend equal rights to women. A year later Congress passed the Civil Rights Act of 1964, which outlawed sex discrimination as well as racial discrimination in hiring and employment.

But so-called "protective" labor laws remain on the books. Limiting the hours a woman can work, or forbidding her to perform certain tasks, these laws have been used as convenient excuses to avoid hiring women for "men's jobs."

In several states, for example, women may not be hired for factory jobs where they will have to lift weights of over 25 or 35 pounds. Yet there are no laws forbidding housewives or domestic workers from lifting 30-pound children, or from moving and lifting heavy furniture when they dust and clean. Nor do laws forbid waitresses to lift heavy trays.

Since the passage of the Civil Rights Act of 1964 there have been many court cases challenging sex discrimination in hiring. In 1971, in the case of Ida Phillips, the Supreme Court said unanimously that refusing to hire a woman because she had pre-school children was illegal if men with pre-school children were hired. But it also said that there might be other cases where an employer could refuse to hire women because of their family responsibilities.

Thurgood Marshall, now an associate justice of the Supreme Court, disagreed with that last point. A hiring policy, he said, must be "neutral as to sex."

In November 1971, the Supreme Court for the first time invoked the Fourteenth Amendment in a case

Ida Phillips of Florida was refused a job because she was the mother of small children—though the same employer hired fathers of small children. Mrs. Phillips went to court to claim that this employment policy is a violation of the Civil Rights Act of 1964.

involving equal rights for women. The Court unanimously found unconstitutional an Idaho law which gave preference to men in administering the estates of people who died without a will.

Under the Fourteenth Amendment some of the rights of mentally retarded people have also been protected. So have some of the rights of people on welfare.

In 1969 a California man asked a public hospital for a sterilization operation to keep him and his wife from having any more children. The couple, who were poor, were entitled by law to free medical treatment.

The hospital and the county health department refused permission for the operation. So the couple went to court and sued. Their lawyers argued that refusal to perform the operation was a violation of their equal rights under the Fourteenth Amendment. The California court agreed with them and ordered the hospital to perform the operation.

Another 1969 case concerned three Ohio doctors. They practiced medicine in a small town in Ohio just across the state line from Wheeling, West Virginia. The only good-sized hospitals in the area were two in Wheeling. These two hospitals refused to accept patients from the three Ohio doctors. They pointed to a hospital rule which said that only doctors who practiced in that same county could use the Wheeling hospitals.

A federal court ruled that the hospitals had to let the doctors use their facilities. The hospital rule, said the court, violated the equal-protection clause of the Fourteenth Amendment. If a doctor can't put his patients in the nearest hospital, the court pointed out, he will have to turn them over to a doctor who can. This gives one doctor an unfair advantage over the other. The hospitals had to abide by the equal-protection clause.

Civil-rights lawyers have begun to use the Fourteenth Amendment in many imaginative ways. In 1969 the NAACP began suit against suburban zoning laws. Such laws require that each new house have a great deal of land around it. Some forbid apartment houses. These laws keep housing expensive in the suburbs, out of reach of poor families seeking to escape from crowded big-city slums. The NAACP charges that such zoning violates the equal-protection clause of the Fourteenth Amendment.

When anti-slavery Congressman John A. Bingham was helping to write the Fourteenth Amendment in 1866, he said its purpose was "to arm the Congress of the United States with the power to enforce the bill of rights."

But well into the twentieth century the Supreme Court said that the Bill of Rights—the first ten amendments to the Constitution—protects people only from the federal government, not from state governments.

In 1925 the Supreme Court began to change its mind. It said that an individual's freedom of speech, guaranteed by the First Amendment, was a "fundamental" freedom. Therefore freedom of speech could not be denied by the states without violating the Fourteenth Amendment. The other liberties listed in the First Amendment—freedom of the press and of religion and the right to hold public meetings—were soon included by the Supreme Court as fundamental freedoms protected by the Fourteenth Amendment.

More recently the Court has used the "due process" and "equal protection" clauses of the Fourteenth Amendment to extend specific guarantees of the Fourth, Fifth, Sixth, Seventh, and Eighth Amendments to the states. In an important decision of 1961, *Mapp v. Ohio,* the Court ruled that the Fourth Amendment applies to the states as well as the federal government—because of the Fourteenth Amendment. As a result of this historic ruling, evidence obtained illegally by the police may not be used in state criminal trials.

The Supreme Court's new mood even brought back to life the Civil Rights Act of 1866—the law repassed by Thaddeus Stevens and other Radical Republicans over the veto of President Andrew Johnson. The 1866 law says that blacks must have the same rights as whites in buying, selling, renting, and using real estate. In 1968 the Supreme Court used the law to require a builder to sell a house to a black buyer.

And in 1969 the Court ruled that a black family who had rented a home in Maryland must be allowed to use the privately owned neighborhood swimming pool. Use of the pool was a legal right of anyone who owned or leased the house, but some white people nearby had tried to keep the black family out of the pool. The Court said that the law of 1866 gives blacks equal rights with whites in the use of property.

Like the Declaration of Independence, the Fourteenth Amendment speaks of equality. But while the Declaration is a hope, the Amendment *is* the law of the land. For almost a century the Supreme Court—reflecting public opinion among white Americans generally—weakened and distorted the Fourteenth Amendment. At times the Court ignored it entirely.

But by the 1970s the Fourteenth Amendment had come into its own. The right of all Americans to be treated equally under the law was now upheld by the Supreme Court.

Unfinished Business

Clarendon County, South Carolina, is one of the places where the school desegregation fight began. When the Supreme Court said in 1954 that Jim Crow schools violated the Fourteenth Amendment it was talking directly to Clarendon County.

Eighteen years later, the schools in Clarendon County were still largely segregated. Most black children were going to the public schools. Most white families either were sending their children to all-white private schools or had moved out of the county to avoid integration.

The Supreme Court cannot enforce its decisions. It can only point out what the law requires. It is up to the executive leaders of government—the President of the United States and the governors of the various states—to see that the law is carried out.

It took U.S. paratroopers with fixed bayonets to enforce the Supreme Court decision in 1957 by getting nine black teenagers into Central High School in Little Rock, Arkansas.

Armed paratroopers escorting teenagers to high school in Little Rock, Arkansas.

It took federal marshals and U.S. soldiers in 1962 to put James Meredith into a classroom at the University of Mississippi.

In Alabama in 1963 the threat of U.S. troops was needed to move Governor George Wallace from a doorway so that two black college students could enroll.

But in many other communities nothing has happened. In many Northern as well as Southern school districts, education is still segregated. In 1971 a federal judge found state and city officials of Detroit, Michigan, guilty of establishing racially segregated public schools.

Black people have discovered that it is not enough for a minority to have an amendment on their side. It is not even enough to have the Supreme Court on their side.

In late 1969, impatient with 15 years of delay and evasion, the Supreme Court unanimously ordered Mississippi and other Southern states to desegregate their schools "at once."

"All deliberate speed for desegregation," said the Court, "is no longer constitutionally permissible." In 1971 another unanimous Court ruling ordered school authorities to end racial segregation. The next steps were up to the President and his Attorney General.

Americans live with other violations of the Fourteenth Amendment. There is still discrimination in housing. There is still discrimination in employment. Black people are still kept from voting in parts of the South. When a black man is accused of a crime, he still has to worry about the fairness of his trial.

Women still face discrimination in employment, in education, in the professions, and in the use and control of property. Because they feel the Fourteenth Amendment does not sufficiently protect them against such discrimination, women's rights leaders have been campaigning for adoption of a new amendment to the Constitution—the Equal Rights Amendment. This proposed amendment says: "Equality of rights under the law shall not be denied or abridged

A student with portraits of two fighters for black rights: Malcolm X (left) and Frederick Douglass.

by the United States or by any State on account of sex."

In the spring of 1971 the Supreme Court refused to rule that keeping poor people out of suburbs by zoning regulations was a violation of the Fourteenth Amendment. Justice Thurgood Marshall disagreed. He said:

> It is far too late in the day to contend that the Fourteenth Amendment prohibits only racial discrimination; and to me singling out the poor to bear a burden not placed on any other class of citizens tramples the values that the Fourteenth Amendment was designed to protect.

What the equal-protection clause of the Fourteenth Amendment says is that each person must have the same rights as any other person. Not all Americans believe that. Hopefully more and more are coming to believe it every day. When a majority believes it, we will be able to live up to the noble words that began our country's history: "We hold these truths to be self-evident: that all men are created equal."

What it will take, as Dr. W. E. B. Du Bois pointed out more than fifty years ago, is "the enforcement of the Constitution of the United States."

APPENDIX

The Fourteenth Amendment

Section 1. All persons born or naturalized in the United States, and subject to the jurisdiction thereof, are citizens of the United States and of the State wherein they reside. No State shall make or enforce any law which shall abridge the privileges or immunities of citizens of the United States; nor shall any State deprive any person of life, liberty, or property, without due process of law; nor deny to any person within its jurisdiction the equal protection of the laws.

Section 2. Representatives shall be apportioned among the several States according to their respective numbers, counting the whole number of persons in each State, excluding Indians not taxed. But when the right to vote at any election for the choice of electors for President and Vice-President of the United States, Representatives in Congress, the executive and judicial officers of a State, or the members of the legislature thereof, is denied to any of the male inhabitants of such State, being twenty-one years of age, and citizens of the United States, or in any way abridged, except for participation in rebellion, or other crime, the basis of representation therein shall be reduced in the proportion which the number of such male citizens shall bear to the whole number of male citizens twenty-one years of age in such State.

Section 3. No person shall be a Senator or Representative in Congress, or elector of President and Vice-President, or hold any office, civil or military, under the United States, or under any State, who, having previously taken an oath, as a member of Congress, or as an officer of the United States, or as a member of any State legislature, or as an executive or judicial officer of any State, to support the Constitution of the United States, shall have engaged in insurrection or rebellion against the same, or given aid or comfort to the enemies thereof. But Congress may, by a vote of two-thirds of each House, remove such disability.

Section 4. The validity of the public debt of the United States, authorized by law, including debts incurred for payment of pensions and bounties for services in suppressing insurrection or rebellion, shall not be questioned. But neither the United States nor any State shall assume or pay any debt or obligation incurred in aid of insurrection or rebellion against the United States, or any claim for the loss or emancipation of any slave; but all such debts, obligations, and claims shall be held illegal and void.

Section 5. The Congress shall have power to enforce, by appropriate legislation, the provisions of this article.

Bibliography

For young readers, the best treatment of the Reconstruction and post-Reconstruction background of the Fourteenth Amendment, and of the major Supreme Court civil rights cases, is in *Tear Down the Walls!* by Dorothy Sterling (Doubleday, 1968). *The Petitioners* by Loren Miller (Pantheon, 1966) is a lively, comprehensive history of the Supreme Court's treatment of blacks for older readers.

For eyewitness accounts, first-hand reports, and other testimony of the times, see Herbert Aptheker's massive collection, *A Documentary History of the Negro People in the United States* (Citadel, 1951). C. Vann Woodward's *The Strange Career of Jim Crow* (Oxford, 1957) is a concise and original analysis of how the Fourteenth Amendment's guarantees were betrayed and black people were kept second-class citizens. For an insight into the Southern white attitude, see W. J. Cash's *The Mind of the South* (New York, 1941).

Evidence of the violence and the legal evasions that led to the demand for the Fourteenth Amendment are found in official reports of the Thirty-ninth Congress (Washington, 1866), in the *Congressional Globe* (Washington, 1866, 1867, and 1868), and in Carl Schurz's *Reminiscences* (New York, 1908). Biographies of Congressional architects of the amendment can be found in Hans L. Trefousse's *The Radical Republicans* (Knopf, 1969) and Ralph Korngold's *Thaddeus Stevens* (Harcourt, 1955). An excellent biography of Stevens for young readers is Milton Meltzer's *Thaddeus Stevens and the Fight for Negro Rights* (Crowell, 1967).

A scholarly and detailed account of the conception and birth of the amendment is *The Framing of the Fourteenth Amendment* by Joseph James (University of Illinois, 1956). For the Reconstruction background, W. E. B. Du Bois's *Black Reconstruction in America* (Meridian edition, 1969) is a major source. More recent studies of Reconstruction are John Hope Franklin's *Reconstruction* (University of Chicago, 1961) and Kenneth M. Stampp's *The Era of Reconstruction* (Knopf, 1965).

The reaction of black Americans to the denial of equality is treated in *The Troublesome Presence* by Eli Ginzberg and Alfred S. Eichner (Macmillan, 1964). For a documented discussion of black thinking and opinion in the era of defeat, see *Negro Thought in America: 1880–1915* by August Meier (University of Michigan, 1963).

Lively anecdotal accounts of the *Civil Rights Cases* (1883) and *Plessy v. Ferguson* (1896) are included in *Quarrels That Have Shaped the Constitution* edited by John A. Garraty (Harper Paperback, 1966). For a scholarly analysis of the origins and interpretations of the Fourteenth Amendment by a legal historian, see *Everyman's Constitution: Historical Essays on the Fourteenth Amendment, the "Conspiracy Theory," and American Constitutionalism* by Howard Jay Graham (State Historical Society of Wisconsin, 1968).

For light on the legal history of the amendment and for documentation of its present broadened application, see Norman Dorsen's *Frontiers of Civil Liberties* (Pantheon, 1968) and *Political and Civil Rights in the United States* by Norman Dorsen, Thomas Emerson, and David Haber (Little Brown, 1967). *The Great Rights* edited by Edmond Cahn (Macmillan, 1963), a collection of addresses by four justices of the Supreme Court, has some useful insights into the Court's more recent interpretation of the "equal protection" clause. *Gideon's Trumpet* by Anthony Lewis (Random House, 1964) is a popular account of an important Fourteenth Amendment case concerning the right of needy persons accused of crimes to be defended by counsel.

Index

Address to the Country (Du Bois), 67
Agee, W. H. R., 34, 42–43
American Federation of Labor, 72–73

Barnett, Ida Wells, 64, 67
Belton, Ethel, 86–87
Berea College, 56
Betts v. Brady (1941), 102
Bingham, John A., 107
Black Codes, 13–15, 25
Blacks
  and ideas of Du Bois, 64–66
  and ideas of B. T. Washington, 58–61, 63–67
  newspapers of, 30, 34, 47, 64, 66
  in Union Army, 5, 7, 33
  as U.S. Representatives, 29–30
  as U.S. Senators, 29
  in World War I armed forces, 68–69
  in World War II armed forces, 77–79
  See also Black Codes; Constitution; Education for blacks; Fourteenth Amendment; Jim Crow laws; Ku Klux Klan; Lynching of blacks; NAACP; Reconstruction; Supreme Court; Voting rights of blacks
Bolling, Spottswood, 86
Bontemps, Arna, 71
Boston *Guardian,* 64
Bradley, Joseph, 42–45
Brennan, William J., Jr., 102–103
Brewer, David J., 57
Brown, Henry, 48–49, 54
Brown, Linda, 85–87
Brown, Oliver, 85–86
Brown v. Board of Education of Topeka (1954), 89, 92
Bruce, Blanche, 29
Buchanan v. Warley (1917), 68, 70–71
Bunche, Ralph, 80

Carnegie, Andrew, 61
Carney, Roddick, 11–12
Chicago *Tribune,* 45
CIO (Congress of Industrial Organizations), 73
Civil Rights Act (1866), 4–5, 19, 23, 26, 38, 70, 98, 107
Civil Rights Act (1875), 30–31, 35, 38, 42–45, 98
Civil Rights Act (1964), 98, 104
Civil Rights Cases (1883), 42–45, 47, 98
Civil War, 4, 11, 15, 43
Commission on the Status of Women (1963), 104
Constitution, U.S., 4–5, 17–19, 39, 57, 68, 80, 113
  See also Fourteenth Amendment; Supreme Court
CORE (Congress of Racial Equality), 96
Credo (Du Bois), 65–66
Crisis (periodical), 70
Crusader (newspaper), 47

Davis, Dorothy, 87
Davis, John, 89
Davis, William R., 34, 42–43
Day, William R., 70
Declaration of Independence, 17, 108
Dickerson, Fayette, 7
Dirksen, Everett, 97
Douglass, Frederick, 3, 10, 45, 59
Dred Scott Case (1857), 18
Drew, Charles R., 53
Du Bois, William E. B., 63–67, 79–80
  as editor of *Crisis,* 70
  and Niagara Movement, 66–67
  quoted, 66, 67, 80, 113

Education for blacks, 30, 53, 58–59, 61
  Du Bois's ideas for, 65–66
  and issue of "separate but equal," 81–91
  during Reconstruction, 28–29

Education for blacks (*continued*)
and segregated public schools, 52, 77, 89, 109, 111
and segregated textbooks, 51–52
Equal Rights Amendment (proposed), 111

Ferguson, John B., 47–48
Field, Stephen J., 40–42, 57
Fifteenth Amendment, 26
First Amendment, 107
Fort Pickering, Memphis, 5, 7–8
Fourteenth Amendment, 19, 46–50, 67–71, 77–85, 88, 92, 96, 100–113
   Du Bois on, 67
   "equal protection" guarantee of, 98–99
   failure of, as protection for blacks, 41–42, 45, 47, 57–58
   and poor people's rights, 113
   purpose of, 40–41, 43, 47–48, 107
   quoted, 23, 31, 114–115
   and racial discrimination, 31, 38
   and Reconstruction, 29, 35
   and Scottsboro cases, 76
   Warren on, 89–91
   and women's rights, 104–105, 111–112
   See also Constitution; Education for blacks; Jim Crow laws; NAACP; Supreme Court; Voting rights of blacks
"Freedom Now!" march (1963), 97–98
Freedom Riders, 96, 100

Garvey, Marcus, 71
Gee, Bird, 30–32, 42–43, 45, 47, 95
Gideon, Clarence E., 100–104
Goodell, Jackson, 5–6
Goodell, Lavinia, 6
Greensboro, North Carolina, 95–96

Harlan, John Marshall, 44, 49–50, 54, 57, 62, 70, 91
Harpers Ferry, 66–67

Harris, Richard, 13
Hastie, William, 80
Hayes, George E. C., 91
Hayes, Rutherford B., 36–38
Higginson, Thomas Wentworth, 33–34
Hoover, Herbert, 71
Houston, Charles, 80
Hughes, Langston, 71
Hugo, Victor, 97
Hunt, Taylor, 6–7

Jim Crow laws
   in courts of justice, 52
   enforcement of, 51–57, 62, 64, 67–68, 71, 77–83, 85, 87–88
   in hospitals, 52
   and issue of "separate but equal," 49, 54, 60, 81–99
   protest against, 92–98
   in public conveyances, 47–50, 54, 92–94, 99
   in public libraries, 52–55, 96
   See also Education for blacks; Ku Klux Klan; Lynching of blacks; NAACP
Johnson, Andrew, 3, 15, 19, 108
Johnson, Lyndon B., 97

Kennedy, John F., 97
King, Martin Luther, Jr., 93–94, 98
Knights of the White Camelia, 8–9
Ku Klux Klan, 36–37

Lewis, John L., 73
Lincoln, Abraham, 3, 43, 61
Little Rock, Arkansas, 109
Lynching of blacks, 57–58, 61–62, 64, 74

McKay, Claude, 71
McLaurin, George W., 83–84
Mapp v. Ohio (1961), 107
Marshall, Thurgood, 80–83, 88–91, 96, 103–104, 113
Memphis *Free Speech,* 64
Memphis *Post,* 8
Meredith, James, 110
Montgomery, Alabama, 92–94, 97

NAACP (National Association for the Advancement of Colored People), 72, 96–99, 102–103
  and enforcement of 14th Amendment, 67–71, 79–84, 88
  and issue of "separate but equal," 68, 81–91
  and Scottsboro case, 75
  and suburban zoning laws, 106–107, 113
  See also Jim Crow laws; Supreme Court
Nabrit, James M., 91
Negroes, see Blacks
New York *Times*, 38, 45, 49
Newspapers, black, 30, 34, 66
  Boston *Guardian*, 64
  Crusader, 47
  Memphis *Free Speech*, 64
Niagara Movement, 66–67
Norris v. Alabama (1935), 76

Parker, John J., 71–72
Parks, Rosa, 92
Plessy, Homer Adolph, 47–48
Plessy v. Ferguson (1896), 48–50, 54, 56, 59, 68, 71, 82–90, 98–99
Powell v. Alabama (1932), 75–76

Reconstruction
  as time of hope, 26–36, 39, 57
  end of, 37–38, 41
Red Record (Barnett), 64
Revels, Hiram, 29
Robinson, Sallie J., 34–35, 42–43, 45, 47
Roosevelt, Franklin D., 74, 80

Santa Clara County v. Southern Pacific Railroad (1886), 46
Schools, see Education for blacks
Schurz, Carl, 15
Scott, Dred, 18
Scottsboro cases, 74–76, 80
Selma, Alabama, 98
Slavery, 4, 27, 36
  and Constitution, 17–18
  Douglass on, 10

  in post-Civil War South, 11–13
  and 13th Amendment, 12, 18
Stanley, Murray, 30–32, 34, 42–43
Stevens, Thaddeus, 16, 20–24, 26, 36, 42, 91, 107
Stoneman, George, 8
Sumner, Charles, 24, 29–30, 36, 98
Supreme Court, U.S., 19, 39–51, 68–76, 80–94, 96–99, 100, 104–105, 109
  and Berea College case, 56
  and 1st Amendment, 107
  and suburban zoning laws, 113
  See also Constitution; Fourteenth Amendment; Jim Crow laws; NAACP
Sweatt, Heman Marion, 79–85
Sweatt v. Painter (1945), 80–85

Taney, Roger B., 18
Taylor, Bob, 7–8
Thirteenth Amendment, 12, 18
Thirty-ninth Congress (1865–1866), 15–16
Tourgée, Albion, 47–48, 50
Trotter, William Monroe, 64, 70
Turner, Henry M., 60
Tuskegee Institute, 59
Tyler, George M., 34, 42–43

Union Army, 5, 33
  15th Colored Infantry, 7
  59th Regiment, 7
  16th United States Infantry, 8
United States v. Cruikshank (1876), 41, 43
United States v. Stanley (1883), 32, 35, 42–43
University of Mississippi, 110
University of Oklahoma, 82
University of Texas Law School, 79–83, 85

Voting rights of blacks, 12, 15–16, 21–22, 57
  and Federal Voting Rights Act (1965), 98
  and 15th Amendment, 26–28
  and 14th Amendment, 23–25, 58
  in the North, 14, 70, 97

Voting rights of blacks (*cont.*)
　in the South, 9, 35, 38, 58, 77, 79, 111

Wade, Benjamin Franklin, 38
Waite, Morrison R., 46
Wallace, George, 110
Warren, Earl, 89–91
Washington, Booker T., 58–67
Washington *Post*, 45
White, George H., 61
White, Walter, 80
Whittier, John Greenleaf, 16
Wiggins, Joseph, 11–12
Wilson, Woodrow, 62–64, 68–69
Women's rights, 104–105, 111–112
World War I, 68–69
World War II, 77–79

Richard Stiller's books for young readers include a group biography of Civil War activists (*The Spy, the Lady, the Captain and the Colonel*) and two biographies in the "Women of America" series. He is also the author of two novels for adult readers, *The Felix Factor* and *The Best Policy*. A former history teacher in New York and Miami high schools, he now lives and writes in Mount Vernon, N.Y.

LARAMIE JUNIOR HIGH
SCHOOL